"GOOD STUFF"

RESOURCES FOR YOUTH LEADERS

VOL. 3

TOPICAL STUDIES WRITTEN BY

RICHARD KOFFARNUS
MOBERLY, MO

PAUL SCHLIEKER
LONGMONT, CO

JIM EICHENBERGER
SPRINGFIELD, IL

WARD PATTERSON
BLOOMINGTON, IN

ILLUSTRATED BY
DAN DUNHAM

COMPILED AND EDITED BY
DAVID P. HENNIG

 STANDARD PUBLISHING
CINCINNATI, OHIO   3411

Key to Scripture references:

KJV—King James Version.

NASB—Scripture quotations marked NASB are from the New American Standard Bible, © The Lockman Foundation, 1960, 1962, 1963, 1968, 1971, 1972, 1973, 1975, 1977, and used by permission.

NIV—Scripture quotations marked *NIV* are from the Holy Bible, *New International Version.* Copyright © 1973, 1978, 1984 by the International Bible Society. Used by permission of Zondervan Bible Publishers.

ISBN 0-87403-066-8
© 1986, The STANDARD PUBLISHING COMPANY, Cincinnati, Ohio.
Division of STANDEX INTERNATIONAL CORPORATION. Printed in U.S.A.

TABLE OF CONTENTS

HEY YOU! READ THIS FIRST!!! 5

REASONS TO BELIEVE, BY RICHARD KOFFARNUS 7

Introduction
Service Project/Social Activity
Session 1: God—Does He Exist?
Session 2: The Bible—Can I Trust It?
Session 3: Jesus—Who Was He Really?
Session 4: The Resurrection on Trial
Worksheets/Script

HOW TO HANDLE YOUR EMOTIONS, ... 43
BY PAUL SCHLIEKER

Introduction
Service Project/Social Activity
Session 1: How to Handle Anger
Session 2: How to Handle Worry
Session 3: How to Handle Insecurity
Session 4: How to Handle Guilt
Worksheets/Transparencies

BEHIND THE SCENES: EVALUATING TV AND MOVIES . . 76
BY JIM EICHENBERGER

Introduction
Service Project/Social Activity
Session 1: TV, Movies, and Your Time
Session 2: TV, Movies, and Your Relationships
Session 3: TV, Movies, and Your Mind
Session 4: TV, Movies, and Your Choices
Worksheets/Transparency/Script

HABITS: MAKING AND BREAKING THEM, ... 114
BY WARD PATTERSON

Introduction
Service Project/Social Activity
Session 1: You and Your Habits
Session 2: Breaking Habits
Session 3: Addictive Habits
Session 4: Making Habits
Worksheets/Transparency/Script

IDEA BANK 149

HEY YOU! READ THIS FIRST!

Because the needs of your group are in a *constant state of change,* you need *flexible material* to meet those needs. **"GOOD STUFF"** has been designed to be used in a *variety of ways* to help you lead your group in the most productive way. This material is *flexible enough* to be used for weekly youth meetings, Bible studies, and discipleship groups, or for retreats, camps, and other special events.

Many of *today's teenagers* are interested in the Bible only as long as they can see it's *relevance for today.* This book provides you with topical studies that will *help your teens get into God's Word.* They will learn Biblical truths and principles as they relate to *issues faced in everyday life.*

All of the studies are outlined in the same manner. Here is an explaination of the features you will find in each study:

* The **Introduction** section will explain the relevance and importance of the topic. It will help you understand the need for this study.

* The **Service Project/Social Activity** section will give you some suggestions for activities that are correlated with the study. These activities will help reinforce what you are teaching.

* The **Sessions** themselves follow a simple outline. The *Objectives* section will explain what the teens will be able to do as a result of their participation. The *Advance Preparation* section will list all of the things you will need to prepare. The *Meeting Schedule* section gives the suggested time schedule. The teaching material is divided into four sections: *Ready,* which hooks the interest of teens into the session, *Research,* which helps teens discover Bible truths and principles, *Respond,* which helps teens apply what they have learned, and *Closing,* which gives suggestions for closing thoughts.

* The **Worksheets/Transparencies/Scripts** section provides *master pages* which may be reproduced to use with your group.

...and especially THIS!!

We have also included a section called the **Idea Bank.** This section contains *additional ideas for service projects and social activities.* These projects and activities were submitted by people who are *actively involved in youth ministry.* Read them, adapt them, and have fun using them as you *watch your teens grow* in their love for each other and the Lord!

We hope this book will become one of your *most valuable resources* as you work with your youth. After all, if you want to *meet the needs of today's teens* in your youth program, then you need some **"GOOD STUFF!"**

REASONS TO BELIEVE

BY RICHARD KOFFARNUS

INTRODUCTION

How do you know there is a God? How do you know the Bible is true? How can you be sure Jesus is more than a good teacher? These are some of the questions teenagers are struggling with every day. Their faith is continually being challenged by their peers, by their culture, by their teachers, and by their own changing roles in life. If they are not well grounded in their beliefs now, their chances of surviving these challenges are not good. The Bible tells us that every Christian needs to know how to defend his faith: "But sanctify Christ as Lord in your hearts, always being ready to make a defense to everyone who asks you to give an account of the hope that is in you." (1 Peter 3:15).

These sessions are based on the book *Why Believe?* by Richard Koffarnus (Standard Publishing, 1981, $2.25). It is suggested that you secure a copy of this book for your personal study. Though only five of the chapters are directly touched on in these sessions, you will want to read the entire book first. You may wish to obtain an additional copy for each member of your group.

Here is an overview of the sessions in this unit.

Session 1

"There is no God. He's just the figment of people's imaginations."

"I believe in God. God is a Force that permeates the entire universe. The Force be with you!"

"OK. *Prove* to me that God exists. Then I'll believe in Him."

One of the basic challenges facing Christians today is to convince non-Christians that there is a God. That may not always be an easy task. Not everyone is willing to accept the same kind of proof.

The atheist may not accept any proof that God is real. His mind is made up. He won't allow you to confuse him with the facts.

The person who believes in a different kind of god requires a different form of proof. You have to prove to him that the Christian view of God is the right one.

And finally, there is the guy who is just not sure. Maybe God does exist, but then again, maybe He doesn't. Let's have some solid proof.

Because of these different viewpoints, Christians have, through the centuries, formulated many proofs for the existence of God. Some have been more convincing than others, but all have met objections.

The purpose of this study is to examine several of these proofs of God's existence.

Session 2

Can we really trust the Bible? Is it actually God's Word? How can we be sure that it is true? Does it matter whether or not today's translations contain mistakes? The purpose of this session is to help teens answer these questions by examining the reliability of the New Testament.

Session 3

The key to establishing the truth of Christianity has always been focused on its founder, Jesus Christ. If we can show that He was really the Son of God, then everything else falls into place. He certainly believed in God. He also believed the Bible is God's Word.

But how do we go about proving His divinity? Historically, the church has always relied on two proofs. The first proof established that Jesus' life was everything the Messiah's life should be. The second proof established the fact that the resurrection proved Jesus to be the living God. This session will deal with the first proof.

Session 4

This session climaxes the unit with a courtroom drama. Can the greatest alleged miracle in the history of the world—the resurrection of Christ—withstand the scrutiny of a court of law? Your youth will become judge, jury, prosecution, and defense as they put the resurrection on trial.

This session is designed to be flexible enough to use many different ways. You can use it as a regular session, just among your teens, or you may wish to present a program before the entire congregation. But if your group is really ambitious, you can turn this program into a ministry project for the entire community. Another alternative in presenting this program is to enlist the help of various members of your congregation. One congregation called upon the local District Attorney to play the role of the judge. Two lawyers played Defense Council and Prosecutor. A real M.D. gave medical testimony about Christ's death. Use your imagination to make your program interesting.

During this study on evidences for our faith, you should become familiar with these two resources of information.

1. Does God Exist?

This is a non-profit organization that was founded in 1968 by John N. Clayton. Mr. Clayton *was* an atheist. He came to believe in God through his study of science and came to have confidence in the Bible as God's Word through his attempts to show it scientifically incorrect. With the interest and support of many people throughout the U.S. and Canada, he is endeavoring to demonstrate that there *is* a scientific basis for belief in God and the acceptance of the Bible as His Word. Mr. Clayton is a public school teacher of physics, chemistry, mathematics, and earth science. He is a graduate of Indiana and Notre Dame Universities holding two masters degrees.

The *Does God Exist?* ministry produces an abundance of resource materials and makes them available to you on a loan basis (all you pay is return postage). If you wish to purchase the materials, they are sold at *production costs!* The materials that are available to you include the following: a free bi-monthly publication called *"Does God Exist?,"* 2 free correspondence courses, video tapes, 16 mm films, filmstrips, books, cassettes, and other printed material.

You are encouraged to write or call for an information packet and to put your name on the mailing list. Some of these materials are recommended for use in the first session, so give yourself plenty of time for planning. Here is the address and phone number:

Does God Exist?
17411 Battles Road
Southbend, IN 46614-9702
(219)/291-9184

2. Institute for Creation Research

The Institute for Creation Research is located in El Cajon, California. ICR is involved in a number of important ministries: education through their graduate school, field research projects including the search for Noah's Ark, speaking engagements at debates and Bible-science seminars, and a museum open to the public and free of charge.

One of the most important goals of the ICR has been the writing and production of sound books, articles, and audiovisual materials related to creation and general Christian evidences. ICR publishes two periodicals, both of which are available for free: *Acts and Facts,* a monthly newsletter; and *Days of Praise,* a quarterly devotional guide. A catalogue of their resource materials for rent or purchase is also available.

You are encouraged to write or call for an information packet and to put your name on the mailing list. Here is the address and phone number:

Institute for Creation Research
P.O. Box 2667
El Cajon, CA 92021
(619)/440-2443

PROJECT/ACTIVITY

The project for this unit is based on Session Four. Have teens organize and present *The Resurrection on Trial* for the entire congregation. Additional details and suggestions for presentation are given with that session. If you decide to do this project, it is recommended that you begin preparing early. Set a date for the presentation—preferably several weeks after you use the session in your meeting. Choose participants early so that they can begin preparing. Please note: this is not a drama in the usual sense. It is not as important to memorize lines exactly as it is to present the facts accurately. As you do your research, you may wish to add or change witnesses or arguments to make the project better suited to the size and talents of your group.

Plan a *cast party* to follow your presentation of *The Resurrection on Trial.* Serve light refreshments and informally discuss the impact of the drama. Was it convincing? Was it accurate? How could it have been improved? In what other ways can you reach out to the lost with this project? Consider the possibility of scheduling performances at other churches, camps, retreats, or rallies.

Close with devotional thoughts on the importance of the resurrection today.

Session 1

GOD—DOES HE EXIST?

OBJECTIVES

As a result of this session, teens should be able to do one or more of the following:

1. Understand that we must always be ready to give a rational defense for our faith.

2. Explain three proofs for the existence of God.

3. Refute an atheists arguments against the existence of God.

4. Evaluate the consequences of belief or unbelief in the existence of God.

ADVANCE PREPARATION

1. Read the book *Why Believe?* described in the unit introduction. If you have read it, reread chapter five to review the topic of this session.

2. Secure a 16mm movie projector and screen or a VCR and monitor if you use the film "Biological Design as a Proof of God's Existence" suggested in the first *Research* activity.

3. Contact a person to pose as an atheist or record the arguments on tape according to the details provided if you use the second *Research* activity.

MEETING SCHEDULE

Ready	10 minutes
Research	30 minutes
Respond	15 minutes
Closing	5 minutes

READY

Before the session begins, write this statement on a chalkboard or poster: *"How can we know God exists?"* When everyone has arrived, ask teens to share their answers. Record their comments in abbreviated form on the chalkboard or poster. Then, share the following thoughts with the group.

"One of the basic challenges facing Christians today is to convince unbelievers that there is a God. *'How do you know there is a God? How do you know the Bible is true? How can you be sure Jesus is more than just a good teacher?'* These are some of the questions we must be ready to answer!

"First Peter 3:15 says, 'But in your hearts set apart Christ as Lord. Always be prepared to give an answer to everyone who asks you to give the reason for the hope that you have' (NIV). This means we should always be ready to give a rational, logical answer to those who would question our faith. The purpose of this unit is to help us understand some of the information that will enable us to do that. During this session, we will look at the evidence that points to the existence of God."

Research

Use one of the following activities to continue this session.

1. Does God Exist?

Order the film "Biological Design as a Proof of God's Existence" from the *Does God Exist?* ministry described in the unit introduction. It is available as a 16 mm film or as a video cassette (VHS or Betamax formats). Show the film for the *Research* section of this session. It lasts about 27 minutes and comes with discussion questions you can use in the *Respond* section. Remember, this resource is available to you on a loan basis. All you must pay is the return postage!

2. Answering an Atheist

Contact a Christian whom your teens do not know (i.e—a preacher from a nearby town). Be sure this person understands the basic atheistic philosophies. Ask him to come to this session as an *atheist* and be prepared to present as many atheistic concepts as convincingly possible.

As you introduce your *guest speaker* to the group, encourage teens to question, challenge, or seek to clarify any statement that is made. The speaker, in turn, should be prepared to answer your group's queries from an atheist's viewpoint.

This activity will allow teens to struggle with the claims of atheists within a controlled environment. They will also have an opportunity to sharpen their thinking as to the arguments favoring the existence of God.

If you are unable to contact a *guest speaker*, you may still want to use this activity with a slight variation.

The statements listed here are some of the most common arguments presented by atheists to refute the existence of God. The rebuttals to these arguments are also provided following each statement. Simply read aloud some of the statements to your group and allow them to provide the responses. Another idea is to record the statements on a cassette tape. Play back each statement and allow the group to respond. Here are the arguments.

Argument 1—"*One cannot prove that God exists.*"

That's true. One cannot prove, beyond a shadow of a doubt, that God exists. But one cannot *disprove* the existence of God either. As a result, one must honestly examine the evidence available: nature, the intricacies of man himself, the historical reality of Jesus and the Bible. When all is said and done, all the evidence points to God. We must then determine whether or not we wish to believe and trust in that evidence. A person who refuses to believe in God has either failed to examine the evidence, or has refused to accept it.

ANSWERING AN ATHEIST

Argument 2—*"If there is a God, why does He allow so much war, suffering, and chaos to exist in this world?"*

The real question here is this, *"Does the existence of God have anything to do with war, suffering, and chaos?"* In the final analysis, the answer is no. Man is responsible for these things, as a result of an item commonly known as *sin.*

This argument is similar to the following: "If my Dad exists, why does he allow me to cuss, smoke pot, get drunk, and speed?" Your dad may well have set rules forbidding you to do any of these things, but you chose to break those rules and do as you pleased. So why blame Dad?

In the same way, why blame God? He created man a free creature, able to choose between right and wrong. Had He not done that, we would be nothing more than flesh-and-bone robots, responding to the whims of an overprotective owner. Because of the freedom granted, man was able to choose whether or not to have fellowship with God.

Man chose to reject God, and allowed sin to separate him from his Maker. As a result of man's sin, many evils such as war, suffering, and chaos have existed in the world. So let's not blame God for the mess *we* have created!

Argument 3—*"How can one reconcile the existence of God with the common proofs of evolution available today?"*

What are the common proofs of evolution? All the *proven* scientific data available to those who espouse the evolutionary view does not cast any shadow of doubt upon God's existence. Archaeology, fossil records, and the like have constantly supported the claims of the Bible regarding God. The various claims speculated by evolutionists, however, have not been substantiated.

Something else must also be remembered. Evolution is no more than an unproven theory. It rests on presuppostions and speculations, not facts. It must be accepted on the basis of faith! There is no evidence that can justifiably cause one to accept evolution conclusively. There *is* evidence for God.

12

Argument 4—*"God is just a crutch."*

The argument presented by this statement stems from the philosophy that claims that man is all-sufficient, capable of doing anything and everything. Those who hold this view have concluded that since man's mind and ability are limitless, God is not needed. Those who do rely on Him are merely using a crutch to satisfy an emotional hang-up.

There are problems with such a view, however. If God is no more than a crutch, and man is capable of solving everything, then why hasn't he taken care of the problems in the world? Why is there still hunger, pollution, social injustice, war, murder, robbery, etc.? Why does the world live in the fear of nuclear holocaust? Why do thousands of people commit suicide each year, claiming to lack purpose in life? Isn't man supposed to be able to eliminate these problems from society?

The Bible gives us a hint of what happens to man when he tries to exclude God from his life. In Romans 1:18-32, Paul tells us that when man turns away from God, the results are catastrophic: lying, idolatry, degrading passions, unrighteousness, wickedness, murder, and more, become a part of the person or society who rejects God. Man's claim to self-sufficiency has fallen far short, and is therefore unreliable.

On the other hand, a proper understanding of the God of the Bible can help man solve the insurmountable problems facing him. God is a crutch only when we treat Him as such—someone to get us out of trouble or to be a personal genie. But the Scriptures and other evidence depicts God as Creator and Lord of all, and He deserves to be treated as such.

The most ridiculous thing about this argument is this—just because someone says, "God is just a crutch" doesn't prove that God doesn't exist. If I approach a friend and say, "Your car is just a crutch," that doesn't prove that he doesn't have a car. This argument, used by atheists, often does not deal with the issue at hand: the existence (or non-existence) of God.

Argument 5—*"No one has ever seen God. If there is a God, why doesn't He show himself to me?"*

This argument is very common among atheists. "God has never shown himself to me; therefore, I don't believe in Him." It is rather interesting that many people are willing to meet God on *their* terms. Yet, when they are challenged to meet God on *His* terms—through His Word—they often refuse. Why?

The wish of the atheist to see God would only result in one thing: death. If God does exist, and He is the God presented in the Bible, then no man can see God and live (Exodus 33:20). Once a person has submitted himself to God and His ways, He can then look forward to eternal fellowship with the Father. Those are God's terms. Why not meet Him there?

Jesus demonstrated to the Pharisees that He was (and is) God's Son through many miracles and other proofs. In spite of the evidence, the Pharisees rejected Him.

Are things any different today?

YOU GOTTA BE KIDDING!?

RESPOND

Use one or both of the following activities to continue this session.

1. Discussion Questions

If you used the film, "Biological Design as a Proof of God's Existence," use the discussion questions that come with the film during this time. Make sure teens understand how Romans 1:19-23 speaks to this issue of the existence of God.

2. Alternatives

Place the following statements on the chalkboard or an overhead transparency. Then allow teens to discuss each of the statements.

1. If you believe in God, Jesus, the Bible, and live accordingly and die, but it turns out that Christianity is only a myth . . .

   a. What have you gained?

   b. What have you lost?

2. If you do not believe in God, Jesus, and the Bible, then find out after your death that Christianity is right . . .

   a. What have you gained?

   b. What have you lost?

Help group members to understand that we, as Christians, have the most to gain and the least to lose by basing our lives on the fact that God does exist!

CLOSING

Ask each teen to share one new thing he or she learned from this session about the existence of God. If you have a large group, you may want to do this in small groups. Then close with a prayer thanking God for making himself known to us through the things that are made!

SESSION 2

[handwritten: —doubts — Does God Exist?]

[handwritten: — written so long ago, i can't be trusted — contradictions]

[handwritten: Bowling — permission slip.]

THE BIBLE— CAN I TRUST IT?

OBJECTIVES

As a result of this session, teens should be able to do one or more of the following:

1. Identify the dates when the Gospels were written.
2. Give reasons for assigning these dates to them.
3. Resolve two alleged contradictions in the Gospels.
4. Make a personal decision about the reliability of the Scriptures based on this study.

ADVANCE PREPARATION

1. Read chapters 12 and 13 of *Why Believe?*
2. You may want to do some further reading on this subject for your personal study. Here are some suggestions.

> Bruce, F. F. *Are the New Testament Documents Reliable?* Grand Rapids, MI: Eerdmans, 1954.
>
> Voss, Howard. *Can I Trust My Bible?* Chicago, IL: Moody Press, 1963.

3. Make copies of Worksheets 1, 2, and 3 from the masters at the end of the unit.
4. Make sure there are Bible dictionaries, and Bible handbooks available for use.
5. Make sure there are plenty of Bibles, four 3 X 5 cards, and pencils available for use.

MEETING SCHEDULE

Ready	15 minutes
Research	20 minutes
Respond	20 minutes
Closing	5 minutes

READY

To begin this session, distribute Worksheet 1. Allow teens about 5 minutes to complete the questions. The questions along with the answers (printed in bold) are listed here for your convenience.

1. The New Testament was written between
   a) **A.D. 30-100**   c) A.D. 200-300
   b) A.D. 100-200   d) A.D. 300-400
2. The earliest complete copies we have of any New Testament book are dated around
   a) A.D. 50   c) A.D. 150
   b) A.D. 100   d) **A.D. 200**

15

3. The New Testament was originally written primarily in what language?
   a) **Greek**   c) Aramaic
   b) Hebrew   d) Latin

4. The total number of known Greek manuscripts (copies) of the New Testament is about
   a) 50   c) **5,000**
   b) 500   d) 50,000

5. Our New Testament text reflects the original document on an accuracy level of
   a) 75%   c) **99.8%**
   b) 87%   d) 100%

6. The apostle Paul wrote at least (choose one) New Testament books.
   a) 5   c) 9
   b) 3   d) **13**

7. The author of the book of Acts is also the author of the Gospel of
   a) Matthew   c) **Luke**
   b) Mark   d) John

8. The author of the Gospel of _____ was a companion of Peter.
   a) Matthew   c) Luke
   b) **Mark**   d) John

9. Which two Gospels were written by apostles of Jesus?
   a) **Matthew**   c) Luke
   b) Mark   d) **John**

When everyone has had a chance to answer the questions, share the following thoughts with the group.

"The Bible is the best place to find proof of God's existence. But how can we be sure that the Bible is true? "Tell them that there are three main questions that must be answered in order to determine whether or not the Bible is reliable?

1. Do we have the original documents or accurate copies of them?

2. Were the originals accurate records of events written by eyewitnesses or from the testimonies of eyewitnesses?

3. Is the truthfulness of the writings confirmed by such areas as secular history and archaeology?

"Because of all that is involved in answering these questions, this study will only focus upon the New Testament, but the principles involved in this study apply to the entire Bible as well."

Distribute Worksheets 2 and 3 at this time. Then, review the answers to the worksheet using the thoughts listed here.

1. The last New Testament book was probably written before A.D. 100, and certainly after the crucifixion of Christ, around A.D. 30. More will be said about this later.

2. We do not have the original copies of the New Testament books, but we do have complete copies of individual books as early as A.D. 200. The Bodmer Papyri, dated about that time, contain the books of Jude, 1 and 2 Peter, and most of Luke and John.

3. Greek was the universal language of the New Testament days. Aramaic was spoken in Palestine at that time, however, and a few lines of the New Testament, such as Matthew 27:46, are in Aramaic.

4. These manuscripts are careful copies, in the original language, of the New Testament. The actual total to date of all the manuscripts and parts of manuscripts is 4969. Most other ancient writings have too few copies to compare to one another.

The oldest complete manuscript of the New Testament to date, is the Codex Vaticanus, dated between A.D. 325-350. Almost as old is the Codex Sinaiticus, A.D. 340.

Also very important is the John Rylands fragment, containing five verses from John 18. This fragment has been dated to A.D. 117 or earlier. That would put it within 25-30 years of the original.

That means we have a fragment of the New Testament within 30 years of its writing, complete books within 100 years, and the complete New Testament within 250 years. By comparing these figures to those of other ancient writings, we can see that the New Testament copies are far superior in this respect. No other copy of an ancient writing is closer than 800 years to its original.

5. Consequently (from #4), we can determine the accuracy of the New Testament. That is, we know that 99.8% of the New Testament verses accurately reflect the originals. Only 40 out of 20,000 verses are currently in doubt. By contrast, Homer's *Iliad* has about 15,600 lines, but 764 of them, or 5% are in doubt.

6. The books of Romans through Philemon are usually ascribed to Paul. From the chart entitled *Chronology of New Testament Books,* we can see that Paul's letters were written between A.D. 50-68, only 20-38 years after the resurrection. His observations about the life of Christ (1 Corinthinas 11 and 15) and the early church (Galatians 1 and 2) are invaluable to our knowledge of the times.

7. Luke 1:1-3 and Acts 1:1 indicate that the same person wrote both books. Furthermore, passages like Acts 16:10 indicate that the author was a companion of Paul. The earliest tradition identifies him as Luke the physician (see Colossians 4:14). When Paul was imprisoned in Rome the first time (A.D. 60-62 or 62-64), Luke was with him. Acts ends without revealing the fate of Paul, meaning it ended before his release from prison. Thus, the date of Acts must be before 64, and of Luke even earlier, since that was the "former treatise" (see Acts 1:1). That dates Luke's Gospel about 30 years after the resurrection.

8. According to the early church father, Papias, Mark was the secretary of Peter (see also 1 Peter 5:13). Many scholars believe that Mark was the earliest Gospel. A recent discovery of an early fragment of the Gospel may date the book as early as 50-55 A.D. Others, following tradition, date the book shortly before Peter's death in 67 or 68 A.D. Either way, Mark wrote only 20-35 years after the resurrection.

Chronology of New Testament Books

Book	Date
Matthew	A.D. 63-66
Mark	67-68
Luke	58-63
John	85-90
Acts	61-64
Romans	56
1 Corinthians	54-55
2 Corinthians	54-55
Galatians	55-56
Ephesians	60
Philippians	61
Colossians	60
1 Thessalonians	50-51
2 Thessalonians	51
1 Timothy	64-65
2 Timothy	67-68
Titus	65
Philemon	60
Hebrews	67-69
James	45-48
1 Peter	65
2 Peter	66-67
1 John	85-90
2 John	85-90
3 John	85-90
Jude	75
Revelation	95-96

9. Matthew and John were both, according to early church tradition, written by the disciples of those names. Also according to tradition, Matthew was the first to write his Gospel. He is also believed to have written it in Aramaic. However, we only possess Greek copies. Still, a date in the 60's for Matthew's work is widely accepted.

Since the discovery of the manuscript fragments by John Rylands, there is no doubt that John was written prior to 100 A.D. Some scholars are now even dating John before 70 A.D.

We can draw two important conclusions from the material covered by these worksheets:

1. There is no doubt that we have accurate copies of original New Testament documents. The manuscript evidence is so strong and the agreement so great between copies that no other ancient document comes even close to matching it.
2. The primary sources of historical information about Jesus—the Gospels, Acts, and Paul's letters—were written by eyewitnesses (Matthew and John) or associates of eyewitnesses (Mark, Luke, and Paul) within 17-40 years (with the possible exception of John) of the events.

Thus, we have answered two of our three crucial questions.

ReseaRCH

Divide teens into groups of three to six members each. Number the groups, and assign the following projects.

Odd-numbered groups should study John 13:21-25, and answer the following questions:

1. What evidence do you find that indicates that this passage was written by an eyewitness?
2. Is there any other possible explanation for your findings? Which is the most reasonable explanation?

Even-numbered groups should study Luke 3:1, 2 and answer these questions.

1. List the names of people and places mentioned by Luke in these verses.
2. Using commentaries and other reference books, evaluate the accuracy of Luke's statements.

Be sure to provide an adequate number of resource books (commentaries, Bible dictionaries, Bible handbooks, etc.) for the even-numbered groups.

When they have finished, call the groups together again and review their findings. Use the commentary below and additional information from *Why Believe?* chapters 12 and 13, to aid the discussion.

John 13:21-25

This passage, like so many others in John's Gospel, shows that the author was an eyewitness of the events recorded, and, most likely, an apostle.

Throughout the Gospel the author distinguishes himself by his familiarity with the events. Only John's Gospel mentions Nicodemus (chapter 3) and Lazarus (chapter 11). Only John identifies the high priest's servant by name (18:10). John also makes eyewitness statements. He speaks of having seen Christ's glory (1:14). John records intimate conversations between Jesus and the twelve (see 6:5-9; chapters 13-16), and among the twelve apart from the Lord (see 4:33; 20:25; 21:3, 7).

But the incidents of the Last Supper are especially indicative of an eyewitness. Luke (chapter 22), Mark (chapter 14), and Paul (1 Corinthians 11) give their accounts of the incident, probably based on interviews with the twelve. And Matthew gives his own eyewitness account (chapter 26). But John gives his narration the special marks of one close to the Master. John 13:21 tells us that Jesus was "troubled in spirit" by Judas' imminent betrayal (see verse 18), a personal observation similar to John's remarks in 11:33, 38. John also notes the solemnity of the occasion by his remark, "Jesus . . . testified, and said. . . ." The Greek term translated "testified" indicates that a serious statement follows. We get an indication of the very tone of voice Jesus had when He said, "one of you will betray Me."

Another indication of eyewitness testimony comes in verses 23-25. The usual arrangement at a Palestinian meal of that time was for the guests to recline on couches arranged in a U-shape around a table. Those dining would lean on their left elbows with their bodies stretched out, away from the table. Their right hands were free to eat with. The host would recline with the two most important guests on his left and on his right. The disciple "whom Jesus loved" (v. 23) would have been on the right, where he could easily lay his head on Jesus' breast. Judas must have been in the place of honor, where he could share the same bowl of sop with the Lord (v. 26). Peter was evidently not far from the beloved disciple, for he could both see and speak to him easily (v. 24). Only an eyewitness could have recorded such details. And John 21:20-24 claims that, indeed, the beloved disciple did write this Gospel.

Luke 3:1, 2   *Check out according to archeological evidence.*

Luke's writings are filled with historical references that are useful to us in two ways. First, they aid in dating his writings. Second, they reflect the accuracy of Luke's writings. The names of people and places mentioned by Luke have been verified by historians and archaeologists, testifying to the truthfulness of God's Word.

Luke tells us in this passage that John the Baptist's ministry began in the fifteenth year of the reign of Tiberius Caesar. Tiberius was the second emperor of Rome. When Augustus died in A.D. 14, Tiberius came to the throne at the age of 56. Thus, thanks to Luke, we know that John began his ministry in A.D. 29, the fifteenth year of Tiberius. At that time, Pontius Pilate was already governor of Judea.

After the death of Herod the Great, king of Judea, in 4 B.C., his kingdom was divided between his three sons, Archaelaus, Herod Antipas, and Philip. Archelaus received the most important part, Judea and Samaria, but he also received the most opposition from his subjects. Eventually, his brutal suppression of Jewish and Samaritan resistance resulted in his exile to Gaul in A.D. 6. To replace him, Rome sent its own line of governors to Judea. Pilate was the fifth to rule, from A.D. 27 to 37. Thus, he was in office two years, by Luke's reckoning, when John began his mission.

Herod Antipas was made tetrarch of Galilee, north of Samaria, as Luke tells us. It was he who put John the Baptist to death.

Philip was given the territory northeast of Galilee, Iturea, and Trachonitis, as Luke records.

Lysanias, tetrarch of Abilene, is harder to identify. Some scholars thought that Luke erred by naming him, but an inscription dated between A.D. 14 and 29 mentions the tetrarch Lysanias. Abilene was a territory north of Iturea. Eventually, the area came under the rule of Herod Agrippa I in A.D. 36. Since Luke wrote after this date, he may have mentioned Abilene to give a complete account of the political climate of the Jewish nation at that time.

One last piece of important historical information supplied by Luke is his mention of Annas and Caiaphas as high priests at the time (v. 2). Annas was made high priest in A.D. 7 and held the office for seven years. Then he was removed from office. His son-in-law, Caiaphas, became high priest from A.D. 18 to 36. Though Caiaphas was the pick of the Romans, Annas was still high priest in the minds of the Jews. So Luke is correct to identify both by the title.

As teens finish sharing their findings, ask them to respond to the following questions:

1. Based on what we have seen, what conclusions can you draw about the accuracy of the New Testament?
2. Should the historical accuracy of the New Testament affect our willingness to believe the doctrine and reports of miracles? Why or why not? (It should. If the New Testament is true everywhere we can test it, we should expect it to be true elsewhere as well.)

RESPOND

There is one last problem to consider. Critics have, for years, accused the New Testament of having internal contradictions. They claim that one Bible writer says one thing, another the opposite.

Bible believing scholars admit that some passages are difficult to reconcile, but they believe there are answers available.

Copy the following questions on a 3 X 5 card (1 question per card). Divide teens into four groups and allow each group to answer the question on their card. Make sure to have plenty of commentaries, Bible handbooks, concordances, and other Bible study helps available for use! Here are the questions.

1. Critics claim the Gospels contradict one another when they record the inscription placed over the cross of Jesus (see Matthew 27:37; Mark 15:26; Luke 23:38; John 19:19, 20). How do we resolve the problem?
2. There are numerous differences between the genealogies of Jesus found in Matthew 1 and Luke 3. How do we explain them?
3. At the feeding of the 5,000, Matthew 14:15 tells us the disciples raised the problem of how to feed the multitude. But John 6:5 says Jesus did so. Who is right?
4. Mark 15:25 says Jesus was crucified at the third hour. John 19:14, on the other hand, says that Jesus was still on trial before Pilate during the sixth hour. Is there an error here?

When youth have had time to develop their thoughts, have them share their answers. You may wish to tabulate them on the board. Below are some suggested answers to the problems. They are not the only answers, but they do show that it is possible to reconcile problem passages without determining that God's Word is inconsistent.

1. John gives us a clue to the problem in 19:20, when he says that the inscription was in Hebrew, Latin, and Greek. It is possible that there were variations in each inscription because of language. It is also possible that some of the Gospel writers (perhaps Matthew and Mark) abbreviated the sayings, keeping the essential message.

2. Several explanations to the differences have been offered. Perhaps the best is that Matthew gives *Joseph's* physical line through his father, Jacob, while Luke gives *Mary's* physical line through Heli. Notice that Luke indicates that Jesus was only "supposed" to be from Joseph (v. 23), emphasizing, perhaps, that He really descended through Mary.

3. The simplest explanation might be that early in the day Jesus brought the problem to the attention of Philip, to set the stage for the miracle. Later, after looking all day for food, the disciples returned with no answer and threw the problem back to Jesus.

4. At least two possible solutions can be offered. One is that the Romans used a time in legal matters that counted hours as we do, from midnight to midnight. If John counted this way, the trial ended at 6:00 A.M. Mark, on the other hand, used the usual reckoning of time, employed by both Romans and Jews, of counting hours from sunrise to sunrise. Thus the third hour would be about 9:00 A.M.

Another solution is that it may be that both writers are simply approximating. John is saying the trial ended "about the sixth hour," that is, it was getting on towards noon. Mark says Jesus was crucified in the late morning.

CLOSING

As this session comes to a close, pose these questions to the group.

1. On the basis of this study, what conclusions have you reached about the trustworthiness of the Bible?
2. In what ways could the information you learned in this session be useful in presenting God to an unbeliever?

Allow just a few minutes of sharing and then close with prayer.

Session 3

Jesus - who was he really?

Objectives

As a result of this session, teens should be able to do one or more of the following:

1. Give two reasons why Jesus could not have been lying about His identity.

2. Give two lines of evidence demonstrating that Jesus was not merely a lunatic.

3. Give two lines of evidence demonstrating that Jesus was actually divine.

4. Evaluate their own convictions about the identity of Jesus.

Advance Preparation

1. Read chapter 8 from *Why Believe?*

2. You may want to do some further reading on this subject for your personal study. Here are some suggestions:

Lewis, C.S. *Mere Christianity* New York: Mac-Millian Co., 1952 (See page 40 and following).

McDowell, Josh. *Evidence that Demands a Verdict.* San Bernadino, CA: Here's Life Publishers, 1979 (See pages 81-183).

3. Make copies of Worksheets 4 and 5, and the script for *The Resurrection on Trial* from the masters at the end of this unit.

4. Make sure there are several commentaries on the Scripture passages to be studied available for use in the small groups.

5. Make sure there are plenty of Bibles, paper, and pencils available for use.

Meeting Schedule

Ready	15 minutes
Research	25 minutes
Respond	15 minutes
Closing	5 minutes

Ready

Contact three men in your congregation and ask them to help you in a *To Tell the Truth* program to be presented to the group. All three men should come to the meeting claiming to be Jesus Christ. One, however, should take the position that Jesus was a liar, the second should view Jesus as a lunatic or madman, the third one, however, should take the position that Jesus is Lord. (*Editor's note:* This activity is not

...and nothing but the truth...

attempting to be disrespectful toward our Lord and Savior. We know that no one can compare himself to Jesus. This activity, however, should be an effective vehicle through which teens can understand that Jesus is Lord. There is no other reasonable alternative on the basis of the evidence.)

Develop a number of questions to be asked of your participants. Your three *Jesus* characters should give their responses to that question on the basis of their assigned view of Jesus. Here are some examples.

Question: Why did you claim to Be God's Son?
#1: Well, I just wanted some attention—so I lied.
#2: How do you expect me to answer that question? I was crazy when I said that!
#3: Because I was—and still am.

Question: How did you succeed in persuading people of your claims?
#1: I lied by telling falsehoods and performing false miracles.
#2: I received my power from demonic sources. I was so insane, I actually didn't know what was going on around me.
#3: By a consistent life-style, miracles, fulfilling Old Testament prophecy, and the resurrection.

Question: Why did you die on the cross?
#1: I wanted to complete the perfect lie in every detail.
#2: I was crazy. I didn't have enough sense to know better.
#3: I died for the sins of mankind, that all who turned to me might have eternal life.

As the activity progresses, encourage teens to ask questions of your special guests. Then, after some time has gone by, have teens choose which person they think answered the given questions in a most consistent and reliable manner.

After thanking the men who helped in this session, ask group members why they chose the person they did. When everyone has had an opportunity to respond, share with them that many people today view Jesus in one of these five ways.

1. Some say He never existed. He is a myth.
2. Others say He was a good teacher, but He never claimed to be the Son of God.
3. Still others believe Jesus was a fraud—a liar.
4. Some say He was a madman—a lunatic.
5. Finally, there are those who believe He was God in a physical body.

Share with the group that in this session we will examine the identity of Jesus.

23

Research

Distribute Worksheets 4 and 5. These worksheets contain an outline of this discussion and some space to take notes.

Share with the group the following material which considers the five positions listed in the *Ready* section. Make sure to use this outline and material as a discussion and not a pure lecture. Spend the most time on the points that hold the most interest for your group. Here is an outline from which to work.

1. **Was Jesus a myth?**
Explore this first possibility with the entire group. Lead this discussion, using the following questions:

a) What reasons might people give for doubting the existence of Jesus?
   1) The character of His biographies could be one reason. Were they mythical or historical?
   2) Insufficient historical evidence might be another reason. Did the ancient historians mention His name? If Jesus were only mentioned in fantastic miracle stories we might think Him a mythical character, like Hercules.

b) What is the character of the Lord's biographies—myth or history?
   Refer to the last session on the accuracy of the Bible. Remind teens that the Gospels are just as reliable, if not more so, as any other book from ancient history.

c) Is Jesus mentioned by any ancient historians outside the Bible?
   Your group members will probably draw a blank here. Refer to *Why Believe?*, chapter 8, for information on ancient historians who mention Jesus.

When you finish this part of your discussion divide the group into three smaller groups of three to six members each. Assign one of questions 2-4 found on the study outline to each of the groups. Provide appropriate commentaries,

if possible to each group. Allow up to twenty minutes for this exercise. If you have more than 18 teens, make additional duplicate groups. If your group has fewer than 9 members, make two groups of three to five each and give each group two questions to answer.

2. **Did Jesus ever claim to be the Son of God?**
The group that receives this question will study key parts of the following passages listed on the outline: Mark 14:53-64; John 9:35-38 (compare Acts 10:25, 26); John 8:48-59.

3. **Was Jesus a liar?**
This group will use these passages to answer this question: Matthew 5:2-11; 7:28, 29; 9:35, 36; John 18:28-38; John 19:32-37; and Matthew 20:18, 19.

4. **Was Jesus a lunatic?**
To answer this question, group three will cover these Scriptures: John 6:14, 15; 10:19-21; 18:1-8; Matthew 27:11-14.

When the groups have finished their investigations, call them back together and review their findings. Use the comments below to aid in your discussion.

2. **Did Jesus claim to be the Son of God?**
Mark 14:53-64

When Jesus was tried, the council had to hastily assemble its evidence against Him (v. 55ff). Numerous false witnesses were paraded before the tribunal. The Old Testament law required at least two witnesses to convict an accused person (cf. Deuteronomy 19:15-20). Both witnesses had to agree on all the facts before judgment could be handed down. The Sanhedrin finally found two men willing to testify against Jesus (see Matthew 26:60, 61), but even their lies did not agree (Mark 14:56-59).

Stalemated, the council had only one hope left: Jesus would have to incriminate himself by uttering blasphemy. The high priest, Caiaphas, challenged Jesus to speak in His own defense. But Jesus was silent (vv. 60, 61). Finally Caiaphas put the question directly to Jesus: "Are you the Christ?" The term "Christ" is the Greek equivalent of the Hebrew term, "Messiah." The Jews believed, correctly, that the Messiah would be the Son of God. They also were convinced that Jesus could not be the Messiah, because He did not correspond to their idea of what the Messiah should be. If Jesus answered the question, "Yes," they would immediately accuse Him of blasphemy, because He would be making himself out to be God.

The Lord knew this, but He still answered the question directly (v. 62). He referred to himself as "the Son of Man," another term for the Messiah, and portrayed himself with two pictures from the Old Testament. First, He would be seated at the right hand of God. The phrase refers to one who sits beside the king as his second in command. Jesus was referring to Psalm 110:1, a passage the Jews recognized to be Messianic in nature (see Acts 2:34).

Second, the Messiah would come on the clouds of heaven. Jesus took this statement from Daniel 7:13, another well known Messianic passage, to speak of His coming to judge Israel.

The high priest immediately recognized the meaning of Christ's declaration. "You have heard the blasphemy!" (v. 64). The council concluded that Jesus deserved death (v. 64). Only Roman law prevented them from passing sentence and executing Jesus themselves.

John 9:35-38 and Acts 10:25, 26

The man referred to in verse 35 was a blind man whom Jesus healed earlier (see 9:1-7). The man was subsequently put out of the synagogue by unbelieving Pharisees (9:24-34).

When Jesus heard that this man had suffered because of his faith, He sought him out. Finding the man, Jesus asked him the critical question, "Do you believe in the Son of Man?"

That phrase "believe on" or "believe in" means "to put one's complete trust in someone or something." Wherever this phrase appears in Scripture, it always refers to either Jesus or God (see John 14:1). It is evident that Jesus was seeking an affirmation of His deity.

Jesus quickly provided the identification (v. 37), upon the man's request (v. 36).

The immediate reply from the former blind man was, "Lord, I believe" (v. 38). John tells us the man *worshiped* Jesus (v. 38)—literally prostrated himself before Him. And Jesus accepted the man's worship.

The willingness of Jesus to accept worship should be contrasted with the apostle Peter's refusal to be worshiped (Acts 10:25, 26). Peter was a follower of Jesus. After bringing Cornelius back to his feet, Peter then proceeded to present the One deserving worship—Jesus of Nazareth, the Son of God. The fact that Jesus accepted worship sets Him apart from His fol-

lowers. The fact that His followers challenged people to worship Him sets Jesus apart as the Son of Man!

John 8:48-59

This passage comes at the conclusion of a lengthy debate between Jesus and the Pharisees (John 8:12-47). Jesus had claimed to come to glorify God and give man eternal life (vv. 50, 51). As a result, the Jews were sure Jesus was possessed by a demon (v. 52). Who did Jesus think He was to claim to give eternal life (vv. 52, 53). Clearly, the Jews saw that Jesus' claim was bordering on blasphemy. No man—not even Abraham—could avoid death. How could Jesus avoid death, or help others avoid it, unless He were God? But that was impossible!

Jesus offered a three-fold reply in verses 54-56: 1) His relationship to God, unlike the Jews', was of a Son to His Father; 2) Jesus knew God and kept His Word—He had a personal relationship to God based on obedience—the Jews did not; 3) Even Abraham had rejoiced at the coming of Jesus (v. 56). The term "My day" refers,

most likely, to the incarnation. Abraham would have seen it as a future hope (Hebrews 11:1, 8-10, 13; Genesis 12:1-3).

This was too much for the Jews. They assumed that Jesus had said *He* had *physically* seen Abraham, not that *Abraham* had "seen" (by *faith*) Him. How could a man less than fifty years old (Jesus was in His early thirties at the time) have seen Abraham (v. 57)?

Rather than correct this misunderstanding by the Jews, Jesus affirmed its incidental truth: Jesus existed before Abraham was born! Not only that, but He existed as the eternal "I Am"—a term used in the Old Testament by God in referring to His eternal nature (see Exodus 3:14).

Incensed by this blasphemy, the Jews tried to stone Jesus (v. 59). But Jesus hid himself and went out of the temple.

3. **Was Jesus a liar?**

Matthew 5:2-11 and 7:28, 29

The effect of Jesus' teaching in the Sermon on the Mount was impressive. The people were astounded because His teaching was not like the scribes'. How was this so? First, because Jesus spoke the truth. The scribes were so steeped in tradition that they weren't focusing on God's commands (see John 14:6; Matthew 5:21, 22, 27, 28, 30, 31-34, 38, 39, 43, 44). Second, He spoke with the authority of God. The scribes were forever quoting other scribes, who were fallible and often contradictory.

Matthew 9:35, 36

Jesus put His teaching into practice. He not only spoke of love and kindness, but He demonstrated it as well. Hypocrisy is a form of lying. Jesus was no hypocrite. He practiced what He preached.

John 18:28-38

When the Jews brought Jesus to Pilate, they knew they had no legitimate grievances against Christ, so they simply made a blanket accusation: Jesus was criminal. No doubt they hoped Pilate would take their word.

Pilate immediately recognized that Jesus had not violated any Roman law. So he told the Jews to handle the matter themselves (v. 31). But they wanted Jesus dead, and only Pilate could do that. To placate the Jews, Pilate agreed to question Jesus.

Pilate's first question gets to the heart of the matter. Was Jesus a king (v. 33)? In order to answer, Jesus had to know the origin of the question (v. 34). If it came from Pilate, the answer was, "No, I am not a king as you think of it—a political ruler." If from the Jews, the answer was "Yes, I am the Messiah."

Pilate's response (v. 35) indicates the latter. But Pilate was not interested in Jewish matters. He only wanted to know if Jesus had broken the Roman law.

To the second question, Jesus indicated that His kingdom was no threat to Rome. Pilate's famous question, "What is truth?" (v. 38), was his way of ending the discussion. If Jesus was a king, he was no threat to the Empire. He was completely innocent by Roman law.

John 19:32-37 and Matthew 20:18, 19

The strongest reason to doubt the accusation that Jesus was a liar is His fulfillment of prophecy. The apostles repeatedly emphasized in their preaching that Jesus fulfilled the Old Testament Messianic prophecies (see Acts 3:18; 10:43). These prophecies were made, even by the most liberal estimate, at least 200 years before Jesus was born. Jesus clearly fulfilled literally dozens of prophecies from the Old Testament. The odds of one man fulfilling all of them by chance is staggering. Jesus could not possibly have manipulated them all, since the completion of many prophecies were beyond His control. There is no way Jesus could have arranged for the Roman soldier to pierce His side with a spear (John 19:34; Zechariah 12:10).

4. Was Jesus a lunatic?
John 6:14, 15

If Jesus were some kind of insane person with visions of establishing a great kingdom, one would expect Him to court the support of the masses. Yet when the people tried to make Him king, He refused.

John 10:19-21

Some of those against Jesus accused Him of demon-possession. Others, however, realized that no madman could perform the works, nor speak the truths Jesus spoke. All He said and did glorified God. A demon would not do that.

John 18:1-8

The picture we get of Jesus' arrest is not of some madman being captured. Jesus was in control of the situation at all times. When He spoke, those who came to arrest Him retreated in awe. At His command, His disciples were released. Nowhere, in the account of the arrest, do we see a raving maniac.

Matthew 27:11-14

Jesus' composure before Pilate amazed the governor. Here was a man on trial for His life. Yet, He gave no defense against all the accusations hurled by His enemies. John 18:33-38 (see earlier discussion) indicates that Jesus did respond to Pilate's questions when they were alone, but again, Jesus was in complete control of the situation.

RESPOND

When teens have finished discussing each passage, ask them to draw conclusions from their assignments. Which views about Jesus can be ruled out? What is still needed to prove Jesus is the Son of God? (See Acts 2:22ff and the conclusion of chapter 8 of *Why Believe?*) Help the group come to the understanding that the identity of Jesus and the validity of Christianity rests on one historical event: the resurrection of Jesus!

Explain that in the next session group members will participate in a courtroom drama that will seek to uncover the truth about the reality of the resurrection. At this time, you should handout the scripts. You will need to secure volunteers or make assignments for the various parts and make any other preparations for the presentation.

CLOSING

Close this session with a period of silent prayer. Suggest that everyone join hands and praise Jesus for who He is! After a period of praise, have one person lead with an audible prayer. With hands still joined, close with a praise chorus like *Jesus, We Just Want to Thank You* or *There's Just Something About That Name.*

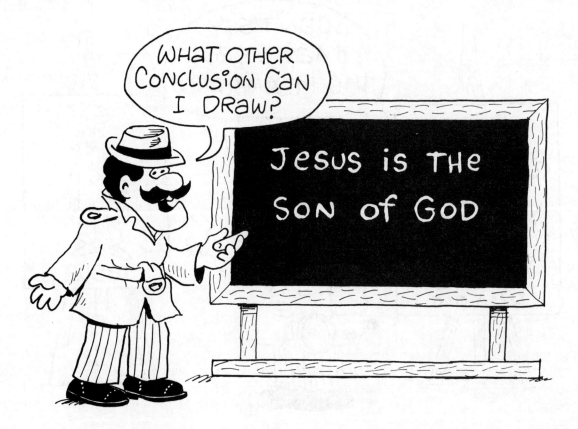

SESSION 4

THE RESURRECTION ON TRIAL

OBJECTIVES

As a result of this session, teens should be able to do one or more of the following:

1. List three facts that prove Jesus actually died on the cross.

2. Refute arguments that refuse to believe that Jesus actually arose from the dead.

3. Make a commitment to God to change one area of their lives in order to live more fully for Him.

ADVANCE PREPARATION

1. Read chapters 9, 10, and 11 from *Why Believe?*

2. You may want to do some further reading on this subject for your personal study. Here are some suggestions:

Morrison, Frank. *Who Moved the Stone?* Downers Grove, IL: InterVarsity, 1958

McDowell, Josh. *Evidence that Demands a Verdict.* San Bernadino, CA: Here's Life Publishers, 1979 (See pages 185-270).

3. Make sure you have extra copies of the script if you let the actors take their scripts with them after the last session. In case some of the scripts do not make it back to the session, you will want to have some extras.

MEETING SCHEDULE	
Ready	5 minutes
Research	35 minutes
Respond	10 minutes
Closing	10 minutes

READY

Before this session begins, rearrange the room to approximate the setting of the trial. As teens arrive, give participants a script, if you have not already done so, and direct them to their proper places.

Explain that the purpose of this presentation is to establish the divinity of Jesus by examining the reality of the resurrection. Help them understand that validity of Christianity rests on the fact of the resurrection. Paul writes in 1 Corinthinas 15:14, "And if Christ has not been raised, our preaching is useless and so is your faith" *(NIV)*. If Jesus' resurrection did occur, it is reasonable to believe that the rest of what Jesus said and did is true. However, if Jesus' resurrection did not occur, then Christianity is false and we have been deceived. The case for Christianity rests in the resurrection of Jesus from the dead!!!

RESEARCH

Have the actors present the drama, *The Resurrection on Trial,* at this time. Encourage teens to be supportive of each other in their roles.

RESPOND

When the teens have responded to the judge by giving their verdict, ask them to evaluate the trial by answering the following questions.

1. Were both sides fairly presented?
2. Were all questions clearly answered?
3. Which side *made its case?*
4. Would this evidence convince your non-Christian friends? Why or why not?
5. What evidence for the death of Jesus impressed you the most?
6. What convinced you that His body had not been stolen?

7. What convinced you that His appearances were not hallucinations?
8. Were there any other objections to the resurrection that should have been answered?

CLOSING

Ask each person to share one thing they have learned in this unit on *Reasons to Believe* that they feel has helped them grow in their faith. If you have a large group, you may want to do this in small groups. Then share the following thoughts with the group.

"During these last four sessions together, we have examined several areas of our faith: the existence of God, the reliability of the Bible, the deity of Jesus, and the reality of the resurrection. While there is an abundance of evidences that give us reasons to believe, the acceptance of these evidences as fact still requires faith. Many who are exposed to these evidences accept them as a basis to a reasonable faith. Still others who are exposed to those evidences steadfastly refuse to believe. Usually, these people do not have an intellectual problem with Christianity—they have a heart problem! They realize that if they accept the existence of God, the reliability of the Bible, the deity of Jesus, and the reality of the resurrection as truth that they will have to change their lives—they will have to start living for God instead of for themselves! Yes, believing does require living a changed life, and that's what the good news is all about!"

Ask each person to pray silently as they make a commitment to God to change one area of their life in order to live more fully for Him.

QUESTIONS ON THE
NEW TESTAMENT

Take about five minutes, and try to answer as many of these questions as you can.

1. The New Testament was written between:
   - a. A.D. 30-100
   - b. A.D. 100-200
   - c. A.D. 200-300
   - d. A.D. 300-400

2. The earliest complete copies we have of any New Testament book are dated around:
   - a. A.D. 50
   - b. A.D. 100
   - c. A.D. 150
   - d. A.D. 200

3. Most of the New Testament was originally written in one of the following languages:
   - a. Greek
   - b. Hebrew
   - c. Aramaic
   - d. Latin

4. The total number of known Greek manuscripts (copies) of the New Testament is about:
   - a. 50
   - b. 500
   - c. 5000
   - d. 50,000

5. Our New Testament text reflects the original documents on an accuracy level of:
   - a. 75%
   - b. 87%
   - c. 99%
   - d. 100%

6. The apostle Paul wrote at least _____ New Testament books:
   - a. 5
   - b. 3
   - c. 9
   - d. 13

7. The author of the book of Acts is also the author of the Gospel of:
   - a. Matthew
   - b. Mark
   - c. Luke
   - d. John

8. The author of the Gospel of _____ was a companion to Peter.
   - a. Matthew
   - b. Mark
   - c. Luke
   - d. John

9. Which two Gospels were written by apostles of Jesus?
   - a. Matthew
   - b. Mark
   - c. Luke
   - d. John

THE BIBLE - CAN I TRUST IT?

A. If we are to trust the New Testament as the Word of God, we must be able to answer three questions:

   1. Do we have the original documents or accurate copies of them?
   2. Were the originals accurate records of events written by eyewitnesses or from the testimonies of eyewitnesses?
   3. Is the truthfulness of the writings confirmed by such areas as secular history and archaeology?

B. The chart below shows that though we do not have the original documents of the New Testament, we can be sure we have accurate copies because:

   1. We have far less time between the originals and their copies than any other ancient documents.
   2. We have more manuscripts to compare than any other ancient writing.
   3. The New Testament has a much higher rate of accuracy than any other ancient document.

Author	Date of Writing	Earliest Manuscript	Number of Manuscripts	Accuracy of Copy
Herodotus	5th century B.C.	A.D. 900	8	_____
Caesar	1st century B.C.	A.D. 900	10	_____
Tacitus	A.D. 100	A.D. 1100	20	_____
Demosthenes	4th century A.D	A.D. 1100	200	_____
Homer	9th century B.C.	_____	643	95%
New Testament	A.D. 30-100	A.D. 200	4969	99.8%

(Dashes in the chart indicate insufficient evidence to make a reasonable estimate.)

C. The chronology of New Testament books gives us important information to use in answering question #2.

Chronology of New Testament Books

		DATE			DATE
Matthew	A.D.	63-66	1 Timothy	A.D.	64-65
Mark		67-68	2 Timothy		67-68
Luke		58-63	Titus		65
John		85-90	Philemon		60
Acts		61-64	Hebrews		67-69
Romans		56	James		45-48
1 Corinthians		54-55	1 Peter		65
2 Corinthians		54-55	2 Peter		66-67
Galatians		55-56	1 John		85-90
Ephesians		60	2 John		85-90
Philippians		61	3 John		85-90
Colossians		61	Jude		75
1 Thessalonians		50-51	Revelation		95-96
2 Thessalonians		51			

From this chronology we can conclude:

1. The primary historical documents of the New Testament were written by eyewitnesses or associates of eyewitnesses of Jesus.
2. The books were written just 17-45 years (with the possible exception of John) after the resurrection.

D. Choose one of the following passages to study, and answer the related questions:

1. John 13:21-25
   a. What evidence do you find that indicates this passage was written by an eyewitness?
   b. Is there any other possible explanation for your findings? Which is the most reasonable explanation?
2. Luke 3:1, 2
   a. List the names of people and places mentioned by Luke in these verses.
   b. Using commentaries and other references book, evaluate the accuracy of Luke's statements.

JESUS–WHO WAS HE REALLY?

To decide who Jesus really was, we must first answer each of these five key questions:

1. Was Jesus a myth?

   a) What reasons might people give for doubting His existence?

   b) Would you call the Gospels myths or histories? Why?

   c) Is Jesus mentioned by any ancient historians outside the Bible? Which ones?

2. Did Jesus ever claim to be the Son of God?

   a) Read Mark 14:53-64. What is the significance of the high priests' question (v. 61)? Of Jesus' reply (v. 62)? Explain the two Old Testament quotes in verse 62 (from Psalm 110:1 and Daniel 7:13).

   b) Compare John 9:35-38 to Acts 10:25, 26. What important distinction can we make between Jesus and Peter?

   c) Read John 8:48-59. Explain Jesus' statement in verse 58. Why did the Jews react so violently (v. 59)?

   d) What conclusions can you draw from these passages?

Permission to reproduce individual worksheets granted.

3. Was Jesus a liar?

   a) Read Matthew 5:2-11 and 7:28, 29. Why were the people amazed by Jesus' teaching in the Sermon on the Mount?

   b) Read Matthew 9:35, 36. What picture do we get of Jesus from these verses?

   c) What verdict did Pilate render in the case of Jesus (see John 18:28-38)? Why?

   d) What two prophecies were fulfilled in John 19:32-37? Could Jesus have deliberately "fulfilled" them? What do these prophecies tell us about Jesus' words in Matthew 20:18, 19?

   e) What conclusions can you draw from these messages?

4. Was Jesus a lunatic?

   a) What was Christ's response to the crowd's efforts to make Him king (John 6;14, 15)?

   b) What was the opinion of those who hated Jesus (John 10:19-21)?

   c) How did Jesus react to His arrest (John 18:1-8)? His trial (Matthew 27:11-14)?

   d) What conclusions can we draw about Jesus from these passages?

THE RESURRECTION ON TRIAL

The dialogue that follows is based on Scripture. Biblical references are supplied in parentheses for later discussion purposes. They are *not* part of the script. The dialogue provided is intended to be a guide. The persons portraying the characters should be free to put the facts provided into their own words.

Setting: A courtroom. A table will suffice for a judge's bench.

Cast

Court Officials: D. John Agnos, Judge
Alan T. Heist, Prosecution
Matthew St. John, Defense
Bailiff
Jurors

Witnesses: Rudolph Shoenmann, Theologian
Caiaphas, the High Priest
A Roman Soldier
David Hartwell, M.D.
Peter
Mary Magdalene

Bailiff (as judge enters): All rise! The People's Court of *(your town)* is now in session; the honorable Judge D. John Agnos, presiding.

Judge: Case #20375, The People vs. The Resurrection. Are the attorneys for the prosecution and for the defense present and ready?

Heist: We are, your Honor.

St. John: Yes, your Honor.

Judge: Very well. Mr. Heist, you may make your opening statement.

Heist (rising, and approaching jury): Ladies and gentlemen of the jury, we have come here today to try a very special case in a very special court. This is the People's Court, where ideas, not criminals, are tried. This is the court of the mind, which decides which ideas are acceptable and which are not.

   Today we have come to disprove a falsehood that has been around nearly two thousand years, and it is high time we did away with it. I speak, of course, of the resurrection of a man named Jesus.

   As enlightened citizens of the twentieth century, we can no longer afford to waste our time on useless myths. Therefore, the prosecution intends to prove, beyond a shadow of a doubt, that Jesus of Nazareth did not and could not rise from the dead. (Sits.)

Judge: Mr. St. John.

St. John (rises): Illustrious members of the jury, you have heard Mr. Heist's challenge: he intends to prove that the resurrection did not and could not happen. The defense in this case intends to prove, on the other hand, that the resurrection is the only reasonable explanation for the strange events that took place in and around Jerusalem at Passover time, about A.D. 30. Because of the unique nature of this court, both prosecution and defense will call on witnesses from the past and present alike. (Sits.)

Judge: Very well. The jurors know the intents of both prosecution and defense attorneys. The prosecution may call upon its first witness.

Heist: The prosecution calls Dr. Rudolph Shoenmann to the stand. (Bailiff swears in the witness.) Dr. Shoenmann, you are a highly respected theologian and New Testament scholar. One of the areas of the New Testament teaching you have specialized in is, as I understand it, the resurrection doctrine. Will you please tell us your view of what happened on Easter morning?

Shoenmann: I believe that Jesus did not die on the cross. He went into a drug-induced trance that fooled everyone. Later, in the tomb, He woke up. When He walked out of the tomb, the guards were frightened away by this "ghost," and He escaped.

Heist: Where did He go?

Shoenmann: Perhaps away to die from His wounds. Perhaps He lived and went into hiding to watch His religion grow.

Heist: So you're saying that Jesus planned the whole thing himself?

Shoenmann: Yes, He even deliberately "fulfilled" prophecy to make it look like He was the Messiah. For example, the whole Triumphal Entry affair was probably staged (Matthew 21:1-9).

Heist: Thank you, Mr. Shoenmann. No further questions. (Sits.)

St. John: Dr. Shoenmann, you said that Jesus was given a drug to simulate death. When did He receive this drug and what kind of drug was it?

Shoenmann: I'm sure there are a number of drugs He could have taken—possibly before, possibly while He was on the cross.

St. John: Well, Jesus was arrested the night before His crucifixion. He was under close guard for hours. He was crucified at 9:00 A.M. (Mark 15:25) and died, or according to you, "went into a trance" at 3:00 P.M. (Matthew 27:46-50). Is there any drug you know of that would have taken that long to knock Him out?

Shoenmann: No. He did receive a drink on the cross, however.

St. John: Yes. The first time it was offered He refused it (Mark 15:23). That drink was laced with painkiller. Later, just before His death, He received a small drink of wine vinegar with no drugs (Mark 15:36). When did He receive a drug?

Shoenmann: Perhaps the drink He took was actually drugged. We can't be sure.

St. John: That wine was given Him by a Roman soldier (Luke 23:36). Was the soldier also involved in Jesus' plot?

Shoenmann: It's possible. Jesus would have needed accomplices.

St. John: If your view is true, yes. But you also indicated that Jesus arranged His own "death" to fulfill Scripture. How did Jesus arrange His betrayal for thirty pieces of silver (Matthew 27:9)? And how did He know the money would be used to buy the potter's field?

Shoenmann: Jesus was an opportunist. I'm sure He saw a greedy tendency in Judas and used it. The others were coincidences.

St. John: What about the gambling for His clothing (Matthew 27:35), the piercing of His side (John 19:34-37), the fact that His legs were not broken, and that He was crucified with thieves (Matthew 27:28)? Jesus fulfilled *all* the Messianic prophecies that were given by the prophets hundreds of years before His birth. The odds against one man fulfilling all those by chance are staggering. How do you explain that?

Shoenmann: Coincidence. Sheer coincidence.

St. John: Very well. Dr. Shoenmann, how do you explain the post-resurrection experiences? (1 Corinthians 15)

Shoenmann: Some of these, I think, were merely wishful thinking or hallucinations by people who wanted to believe that Jesus was alive. Others were probably outright fabrications.

St. John: In other words, you believe that Jesus lied and His followers dreamed up fantastic stories. But one question remains unanswered: Why were Jesus and His followers willing to *die* for those lies? (Pause.) Thank you Dr. Shoenmann. You may step down.

Heist: The prosecution calls the high priest, Caiaphas to the stand. (Caiaphas takes the stand. Bailiff swears him in.) Mr. Caiaphas,

would you please tell us what happened from the time Jesus was crucified until the time the body disappeared?

Caiaphas: Well, after the Romans nailed Him to the cross the teachers of the law, the elders, other Jewish leaders, and myself stayed to observe His death (Matthew 27:41). We wanted to be sure that His body was not left on the cross over the Sabbath. That would have been in violation of the Law (John 19:31). Jesus died around 3:00 in the afternoon (Matthew 27:46). Some of His friends claimed the body and placed it in a new tomb owned by Joseph of Arimathea. That was late Friday afternoon, the day of the execution (Matthew 27:57-60). The next day we got Pilate to seal the tomb and place a guard before the tomb (Matthew 27:64-66).

Heist: Why did you do that?

Caiaphas: We remembered that Jesus claimed He would rise from the dead. We did not want His body stolen so His words might be "fulfilled" (Matthew 27:62-64).

Heist: Mr. Caiaphas, do you know what happened to the body?

Caiaphas: I believe Jesus' disciples stole it, of course.

Heist: Thank you. Your witness. Mr. St. John. (Sits.)

St. John: Mr. Caiaphas, was Jesus dead when His body was taken off the cross?

Caiaphas: Yes, I'm sure He was. He had lost so much blood from the Roman flogging, the crown of thorns, and the spikes that pierced his hands and feet (Matthew 27:26-30). Then there was the spear wound in His side. One of the soldiers was going to break Jesus' legs, so He would die faster. Jesus already looked dead, however, so the soldier pierced His side, just to be sure (John 19:33, 34). He was dead, all right. A Roman centurion certified that fact (Mark 15:44, 45).

St. John: You said the disciples stole the body. How do you know that?

Caiaphas: Who else would? Not us, I assure you. If we had, we would have produced the body long ago and put an end to this non-

sense. Those eleven troublemakers took the corpse. The Roman guards told us so.

St. John: Thank you, Mr. Caiaphas. I have no more questions. (Caiaphas leaves.)

Heist: The prosecution calls the Roman soldier to the stand. (The Roman soldier takes the stand. The Bailiff administers the oath.) Soldier, you were assigned to guard the tomb of Jesus, were you not?

Roman Soldier: Yes sir. The boys and I were sent by the governor to watch this tomb. The Jewish leaders were really worried about someone stealing His body.

Heist: But you failed at your duty.

Soldier: Yes. We-uh—fell asleep on the job. When we awoke, the disciples of Jesus had stolen His body. The tomb was empty.

Heist: Thank you. No more questions. Your witness. Mr. St. John. (Sits.)

St. John: Soldier, you said the body was stolen while you slept. The stone in front of the grave was heavy, wasn't it?

Soldier: Yes sir. It was (Mark 16:4).

St. John: You heard Dr. Shoenmann. Could Jesus have moved the stone if He were alive.

Soldier: No, sir. It would have taken several men to do it.

St. John: How could you have slept while someone rolled away that stone?

Soldier: I guess I'm just a sound sleeper.

St. John: I see. And the other guards are sound sleepers too I suppose. You say you slept while the body was stolen by the disciples. How do you know who took it if you were asleep? How do you even know it was stolen?

Soldier: Well . . . who else could have taken it? It must have been stolen by someone!

St. John: Soldier, I understand that falling asleep on guard duty is a serious offense— punishable by death under Roman law. Why weren't you put to death for neglecting your duty? (Matthew 28:11-15).

Soldier: I don't know, sir. Just lucky I guess.

St. John: Did the chief priests bribe you to say

the body was stolen and protect you from the governor?

Soldier: I wouldn't know, sir.

St. John: Thank you. You may step down.

Heist: The prosecution rests.

St. John: If it pleases Your Honor, the defense would like to call Dr. David Hartwell to the witness stand. (Dr. Hartwell takes the stand. The Bailiff swears him in.) Dr. Hartwell, you are a medical doctor specializing in pathology, are you not?

Dr. Hartwell: Yes, I have been a pathologist for twenty years.

St. John: Will you please describe the wounds Jesus received prior to and during the crucifixion?

Dr. Hartwell: According to the Gospel records, Jesus received multiple lacerations from a flogging by the Roman soldiers (Matthew 27:26). Jewish law limited such punishment to 40 lashes. The Romans had no limitations, so we may take 40 lashes as a conservative estimate. Then He received multiple bruises from a beating with fists (Mark 14:65) and with a reed (Matthew 27:30). His head punctured by a crown of thorns (Matthew 27:29). Finally, He receive five puncture wounds from the nails through His hands and feet (John 20:25) and from a spear thrust into His side (John 19:34).

St. John: Would these wounds have been enough to kill Him?

Dr. Hartwell: Yes, I believe so. From the time of His flogging until He was taken from the cross, over six hours, Jesus bled from numerous wounds. Also, the strain of His own weight, hanging on the cross, would have made breathing extremely difficult for Him. Jesus probably suffered from traumatic shock because of His ordeal. Any one of these three factors or all three combined could have caused His death.

St. John: Would you please explain John's observation of blood and water from Jesus' side (John 19:34)?

Dr. Hartwell: That's hard to explain. Some physicians believe the spear thrust pierced the pericardial bag around the heart. The "blood and water" would actually be blood which had separated into a clot and serum. If that were true, the cause of Jesus' death would have been a ruptured heart. However, we do not know which side of Jesus' body was pierced by the spear. The water may have come from His stomach. In either case, it seems certain to me that the spear thrust would have killed Jesus had He not been already dead (John 19:33).

St. John: Thank you. Your witness, Mr. Heist.

Heist: Doctor, how much blood can a person lose and survive?

Dr. Hartwell: That's hard to say. It depends on the person.

Heist: Could someone have survived Jesus' ordeal, had He been given prompt care?

Dr. Hartwell: It is highly unlikely. However, no one could have survived the spear thrust, if it pierced the heart.

Heist: If it pierced the heart. Thank you. That's all.

St. John: The defense would like to call Peter to the stand. (Peter approaches the witness stand. The Bailiff swears him in.) Peter, we have heard a serious charge against you and the other disciples from two sources. Did you participate in the theft of the body of Jesus?

Peter: Certainly not. Stealing a body was the last think I had in mind. I was convinced that Jesus had failed us. He was supposed to be the Messiah, but He let himself be killed without a fight (John 18:1-8).

St. John: What about the rest of the disciples?

Peter: They felt the same way. We were even afraid to claim the body after He died. If Joseph of Arimathea hadn't, I don't know what would have become of it. No one even considered stealing Jesus' body—we would have been unable to get past the guards.

St. John: You claim to have seen Jesus since His resurrection (John 20:19, 20). How do you respond to Dr. Shoenmann's claim that you hallucinated?

Peter: I'm no psychologist. All I know is that I saw Christ—not once, but several times

(John 20:19-26; 21:1). We all did. We touched Him (Luke 24:39). We ate with Him (John 21:13-15). We saw Him ascend into Heaven (Acts 1:9). He was alive all right. But He didn't just recover from His wounds. His body was changed. He could appear and disappear at will (John 20:19, 26). He was different. But He was still Jesus.

St. John: Thank you. Your witness, Mr. Heist.

Heist: Peter, isn't it true that Jesus predicted His own death and resurrection (Matthew 16:21)?

Peter: Yes, many times.

Heist: After He died, weren't you waiting for His return?

Peter: No. We didn't understand how that could be (John 20:9). We didn't even believe Mary Magdalene when she saw Him (Mark 16:10, 11), until we saw Him, too (Mark 16:14).

Heist: What did you think when you heard the body was gone?

Peter: Total disbelief. I had to run to the tomb and see it with my very eyes. When I saw the tomb, I realized one thing: no one could have stolen the body.

Heist: Why not?

Peter: Because of the graveclothes. They were still there, wrapped neatly (John 20:6, 7). Why would anyone unwrap the body? And even if they did, the clothes would have been torn. You see, burial spices make the clothes stick to the body. They would have been torn up had they been unwrapped. But they weren't.

Heist: I see. No further questions.

St. John: The defense calls its last witness, Mary Magdalene. (Mary approaches the witness stand. The Bailiff swears her in.) Mary, I understand you were the first to see Jesus after the resurrection. Please tell us what happened.

Mary: After finding the empty grave, I ran back to tell Peter and the rest that the body was gone. Peter, John, and I ran back and they looked into the tomb themselves. Then they left, not sure what had happened, I guess.

I turned around and saw this man standing there. I thought He was the gardner. Then He spoke to me and I knew it was Jesus. He told me to tell the others He was alive, and that He was going to ascend to the Father (John 20:10-18).

St. John: Are you sure this wasn't a wishful vision?

Mary: No. I *touched* Him. I *hugged* Him. I *know* He was real.

St. John: Did the others believe you?

Mary: No (Mark 16:11). They did not believe until they saw Him, too (John 20:19, 20).

St. John: Thank you, Mary. I have no further questions. Your witness Mr. Heist.

Heist: Miss Magdalene, how long did this appearance of Jesus last?

Mary: A few minutes, I guess.

Heist: Isn't it true that you really wanted to see Jesus again?

Mary: Yes, certainly.

Heist: Isn't it possible that you *imagined* you saw Him? You wanted to see Him so badly that you thought He was there, but He wasn't.

Mary: No! I *touched* Him. We all did sooner or later. Over 500 of us saw Him at once (1 Corinthians 15:6). That was no vision.

Heist: Isn't it true that you simply invented your story? Aren't all the resurrection stories, in fact, just stories?

Mary: No! You talked to Peter. You know he was killed later because of his faith. So were James and Paul and the rest of the apostles, except John. Would they all die for a lie? Would they suffer imprisonment and deprivation and floggings for a lie?

Heist: That will be all, Miss Magdalene.

St. John: The defense rests its case, Your Honor.

Judge: Very well, you may present your final summation. Mr. Heist, you may go first.

Heist: Ladies and gentlemen of the jury, we have heard a fantastic story here today. A man was crucified nearly 2,000 years ago. We are asked to believe that this man definitely died, though no doctor certified it, that He then defied the laws of nature and returned to life, and appeared to a multitude of people—all of whom were His followers!

I ask you, can we in the twentieth century believe such a tale? Or is it not much more likely that Jesus was stolen from the tomb by His own followers to make Him appear to be a god? Jesus was a clever man. There is no doubt about it. Clever enough to devise this entire plot and carry it out. But not clever enough to fool us! (Mr. Heist is seated.)

St. John: Mr. Heist is right. There was a plot connected with Jesus' death. But the plot was devised by the chief priests and other Jewish leaders. They rigged the trial of Jesus to insure His death. They bribed the guards to say that the body had been stolen. Finally, they spread the story that the disciples stole the body. Clever, isn't it?

We are also told by modern critics that Jesus survived flogging, His crucifixion, a spear thrust in His side, and three days in a tomb. Then He rolled away a massive stone, unwrapped himself from His grave clothes without tearing them, scared away the guards, and convinced His followers He was still alive and bound for Heaven.

We are also asked to believe that Jesus' body was stolen by His disciples (who incidentally, were frightened, confused men), under the noses of Roman guards, and *without* tearing the graveclothes. And then these thieves willingly died for what they knew was a lie.

No, there is only one reasonable alternative. Jesus *did* rise from the dead. Our twentieth century mentalities may not want to admit it, but the evidence presented through history leaves us with no alternative but to accept it. (Mr. St. John is seated.)

Judge: Well, you have heard the evidence presented. Did Jesus rise from the dead or not? You must decide for yourselves. You are all part of the jury. What is your verdict?

HOW TO HANDLE YOUR EMOTIONS

BY PAUL SCHLIEKER

INTRODUCTION

This unit is designed to teach teens how to handle some of their emotions. All people are emotional creatures. One does not have to be very old to realize that his emotions can sometimes get him into trouble. As Christians, we know that God wants us to control our emotions. By doing this we can respond in ways that would please Him, whatever the circumstances.

The basic focus of these sessions is that *strong emotions block rational thinking*. Whether it be anger, worry, a insecurity, or guilt, any emotion can cause a person to think incorrectly. Our behavior, our perceptions, our attitudes, are all affected by any strong emotion. This is true whether the emotion is negative or positive. When a person worries he can think of all kinds of things that are not based on reality. On the other hand, love, joy, peace, and the other fruit of the Spirit are strong emotions as well. These emotions can motivate a person to do what is right just as the wrong emotion can mislead and deceive him.

As you study this material together, continually remind teens that overcoming emotional tendencies takes time. No one can become a calm, peaceful, tranquil, unencumbered person overnight—particularly when he has been known to be a constant worrier for over 15 years. It isn't going to be that easy. Regardless of the emotion, however, Christ *can* be Lord of all—including our emotions. Through His Word, the Holy Spirit, the support of other people, and time, change can take place.

Service Project

Plan a time for teens to visit some people who need emotional support. This could involve the residents of an orphanage, a rest home, or the shut-ins of your congregation.

Be sure to make the necessary arrangements for this project. If you go to an orphanage or rest home, gain permission from the administration of the place you select. If you plan to have teens visit the shut-ins from the church, ask the shut-ins if they can come.

Before the young people are ready to go out on this service project, encourage them to have something planned to do with the person with whom they will visit. If they are visiting orphans, encourage them to take some games. If visiting the elderly, take some table games or some books to read aloud to them. Ask teens to look for the emotions displayed by the person they are visiting.

After the visit, invite teens to your house for refreshments. While you're together, ask them to share the emotions they encountered during their visits. Discuss the following question: "What kind of responses could we give to the people we met today that would express God's love and concern for them?"

As young people come up with suggestions, write them down. Then discuss specific ways your group can begin to implement some of these ideas.

Social Activity

Some of the strongest feelings in the life of a teenager are experienced with his parents. Young people often express anger toward their parents. Parents often worry about their teens. Many young people experience guilt because they have disobeyed or shown a lack of respect toward their father and/or mother. Parents, on the other hand, often feel guilty because they know they could have done a better job in raising their kids.

Consider the following social idea as you further challenge teens to apply the truths presented in this unit of study. Plan with your youth a parent appreciation time. This could be developed as a special recognition Sunday, a banquet, a picnic, a hayride—or anything else you decide.

Be sure to plan this event well ahead of time. If you want adults, as well as youth, to participate in an activity, you *must* give them enough advance notice so they can incorporate it into their schedules. Be sure you and your youth know exactly what is going to happen throughout the time you have planned for this activity. Have games, entertainment, meals, etc., ready for the event. Be sure to have your youth work on developing and carrying out the activity. The event will take on a special meaning for them and their parents.

Toward the end of the activity, inform parents and teens that there is going to be a "Bragging Time." Go around the room and allow all the parents present to brag about their kids. Then go around and allow all the teenagers to brag about their parents. This activity will help solidify family bonds, and open any communication channels that might be *stopped up* at the time.

Close this social activity with a brief devotional thought, challenging both parents and children to allow God—not their emotions—to control their dealings with each other.

Session 1

HOW TO HANDLE ANGER

1, 2, 3, 4, 5, 6, 7, 8, 9, 10

OBJECTIVES

As a result of this session, teens should be able to do one or more of the following:
1. Identify four causes of anger.
2. Identify four ways people handle anger.
3. Ask God's help in controlling one area of their lives in which they are prone to get angry.

ADVANCE PREPARATION

1. Make copies of Worksheets 1 and 2, and Transparency A from the masters at the end of this unit.
2. You will need one or two accomplices to pull off the first *Ready* activity if you choose to use it.
3. Secure an overhead projector and screen for use with the transparency in the *Respond* section.
4. Be sure there are plenty of Bibles, paper, and pencils available for use.

MEETING SCHEDULE

Ready	10 minutes
Research	20 minutes
Respond	25 minutes
Closing	5 minutes

RESOURCE MATERIAL

The Bible has a great deal to say about the subject of anger. Christians are commanded to keep their anger under control. They are to do so because they are to be imitators of God, and God controls His anger. The Bible generally regards God's nature to be "slow to anger, abounding in love" (Psalm 103:8, *NIV).* The Bible, however, does not fail to record instances where God was angry. One of the most well-known occurrences of God's anger is found in

Exodus 32. Moses was about to come down from Mt. Sinai with the Ten Commandments. In the meantime, Aaron and the children of Israel had built a golden calf and had begun worshiping it. As a result of their sin, God told Moses, "Now leave me alone so that my anger may burn against them and I may destroy them" (Exodus 32:10, *NIV*). In the New Testament, we also learn that unrighteousness makes God angry (see Romans 1:18ff).

We must remember, however, that God's anger is always directed toward the *sins* of people, not the people themselves. This truth can be seen in the life of Jesus when He cleansed the temple (see John 2). Jesus was disturbed that the Jews had turned God's temple into a marketplace. He became angry, and overturned the tables and scattered the money. This is an example of what we have come to call "righteous anger."

The basic characteristics of righteous anger are as follows.

1. Righteous anger is a controlled anger. Jesus did act with force when He cleared out the temple. However, He did not lose control of himself.
2. Righteous anger does not harbor hatred or resentment.
3. Righteous anger has an unselfish motivation. Jesus did not exalt himself by driving out the money-changers. He taught them a lesson about reverence.
4. Righteous anger is directed toward actions or situations, not people. God's anger in Exodus 32 was directed toward the idolatry of His people, not toward the children of Israel themselves. John 3:16 says that "God so loved the world that he gave his one and only Son" *(NIV)*. God is angered by sin, yet He loves the people who commit those sins.
5. Righteous anger leads to a positive action which attempts to correct the wrongdoing. Human anger usually turns into revenge. Righteous anger is not that way.

46

One of Jesus' teachings about anger is found in Matthew 5:21-26. In this section of the Sermon on the Mount, Jesus reminded His listeners of the deeper meaning of the commandment, "Thou shalt not kill" (Exodus 20:13). Jesus emphasized that the source of murder was the anger in a man's heart. We learn in 1 John 3:15 that, "Everyone who hates his brother is a murderer; and you know that no murderer has eternal life abiding in him" *(NASB)*. In Luke 15:28, the older brother became angry and would not welcome home the prodigal son. His anger prevented him from acting in accordance with the will of his father—and thus with the will of God. "The anger of man does not achieve the righteousness of God" (James 1:20, *NASB*).

The Scripture passage chosen for this session is Ephesians 4:26, 27. The apostle Paul warns us not to let our anger turn into sin. Anger becomes sinful when we nurse a grudge or hold our bitter feelings within us for days, weeks, or months. Paul says that the sooner we can get rid of our anger, the better. The longer we hold in our anger, the more we give the devil an opportunity to affect our lives.

YOUR EXAMPLE

As a leader, you will likely have had more experience in dealing with anger than your young people, simply because you have lived longer. Sharing times in your life when you responded incorrectly and got angry might be appropriate in this session. Sharing your faults and needs in this area may help teens open up. You may want to share a time when you handled your anger both rightly *and* wrongly.

ANGER IN YOUNG PEOPLE

Every person in the youth group where you serve probably has been angry at one time or another. In dealing with your youth, keep in mind that all anger is based upon what we consider to be "our rights." Every time we feel that one of "our rights" has been violated, we get

angry. The solution to this anger is to surrender our rights to God. This sounds simple, but it isn't. It is rather simple to talk about surrendering our rights to Jesus—it is extremely difficult to put such talk into practice in everyday living. Jesus surrendered all His rights to God. Thus, He prayed while on the cross instead of getting angry: "Father forgive them; for they do not know what they are doing" (Luke 23:34, *NASB).* Many times, when a young person gets mad, one of his rights has been violated. Your youth may not be aware of this principle, but it is certainly true.

Another factor related to anger in young people is the home environment from which they come. Some young people live in "high voltage homes." These homes have very "explosive" members who become angry at the least word or incident. The Scriptural principle involved here is that *like* begets *like* (see Luke 6:40). Angry parents usually produce angry kids. An angry home produces angry family members. When living in such environments where anger is so prevalent, it becomes difficult for young people to respond to situations in a loving manner. Point out that responding in anger to family members never produces the desired result. An angry response never solves a problem; it only makes it worse.

a HIGH-VOLTAGE HOME

IT Takes Time

Stress to your group that it will take time to overcome tendencies to become angry at petty situations. Habits are hard to overcome. But as we focus on God's will, His Word, His love, and His forgiveness, we can "chip away" our habits and begin to overcome our tendency to become angry.

Session Plan

Ready

Choose one of the following activities to begin this session.

1. Fight Dramatization

Stage a fight between two young people or between yourself as the leader and another young person. Inform those who will be involved several days before this session. Be sure they convey to the rest of the group what they are angry about. Make it appear to be an impromptu "fight." Do this as the rest of the group is informally talking. Make sure that the issue being fought about is realistic. This should not last more than a minute. End the dramatization by having one person stomp out of the room. Lead into the input section of this session by sharing the following thoughts.

"Just to ease everyone's mind, this scenario has been staged. The participants (give names) are not really mad at each other. However, they illustrated well what we sound like when we become angry. In this session, we want to talk about anger. You may have heard it said that a Christian should never get angry. But Christians do get angry! We're going to look at a couple of verses in the Bible that speak to this issue."

2. Debate

Write this statement on a chalkboard, poster, or transparency to be displayed before the group: *A Christian should never get angry.*

Divide the teens into two groups. Assign one group to affirm the statement and the other to deny it. Allow each group three minutes to prepare their presentation. Then give each side three minutes to argue their case. After both sides have a chance to present their arguments, move into the *Research* section by sharing the following thoughts.

"This statement you just worked on has been debated by Christians for years. In this session, we're going to examine anger as an emotion that the Christian is commanded to handle."

RESEARCH

WHAT DOES THE BIBLE SAY?

Share the following thoughts with your group.

"While the Bible has much to say about the subject of anger, we are going to focus on just one passage: Ephesians 4:26, 27."

Distribute Worksheet 1. Have three teens read the different versions of the Scripture found on the worksheet to the group. Then, divide teens into small groups of 3 or 4. Instruct each group to find at least three things this passage teaches about the subject of anger. Allow approximately five minutes. Then, call for feedback. List the responses on an overhead transparency or on the chalkboard.

FOUR CAUSES OF ANGER

While teams are still in the small groups, hand out Worksheet 2. Tell them that each of the cartoon strips illustrates one of the four causes of anger listed at the top of the worksheet. Instruct them to read the cartoons

together and identify the cause of the anger expressed by each of the characters. The correct answers are given here for your convenience: the first cartoon illustrates *frustration;* the second cartoon illustrates *injustice;* the third cartoon illustrates *pain;* the fourth cartoon illustrates *selfishness.*

After teens have shared their answers with others, ask them if they can think of any other reasons why people become angry. Then, ask them to share in their small groups which of the reasons mentioned on the worksheet and in their discussion they identify with the most.

RESPOND

Project Transparency A on the screen where it can be seen by everyone. Then share the following thoughts with your group.

"In his book, *The Christian Use of Emotional Power,* Norman Wright states that there are four common ways in which people deal with their anger. They are listed on this transparency. When one *represses* anger, he fails to admit that he is angry. This would be the person who would be obviously angry but would say, 'No, I'm not angry.' To *suppress* anger, a person must know he is angry, but he will not let it show.

Suppressing our anger is something we commonly do when we are in public—at work, in school, or in a crowded shopping center. A person who chooses to *express* his anger blurts out his feelings, and fails to take into consideration the feelings of others. This is a common reaction of a small child. A person who chooses to *confess* his anger must first acknowledge that he is angry to himself, to God, and to the other person involved. *Confession* does take into consideration how another person might feel. In talking to another person about our anger we must never say, *'You* made me angry.' Other people do not control the way we feel. *We* are in control of our own emotions. *We* choose whether or not we become angry at something or someone. A more appropriate statement might be something like this: *'What's happening here is making me angry. Could we talk about it?'"*

SKITS

Instruct the small groups to develop a short skit that would illustrate the different responses to anger just mentioned. Have each group illustrate a different response. Allow four minutes for the groups to prepare. Then have them present their skits.

DISCUSSION QUESTIONS

Instruct the teens to refer back to the discussion questions on Worksheet 1. Lead a discussion with the entire group on these thoughts. The questions along with possible answers are listed here for your convenience.

1. *What steps could a person take to overcome anger?* Read selected Scriptures about anger. Pray for the person who makes you angry. Discuss your anger with the person involved.

2. *How could you confront a person who is quick to get angry or prone to hold grudges?* We must first be sure that we have earned the right to confront them about their anger. We can earn this right by building a strong friendship with that person—a friendship that always conveys acceptance and love *for the person,* though we may not condone their actions. If a person is quick to get angry, we may need to suggest to them that they are "wearing their emotions on their sleeves"—that is, they are taking everything too personally—and they need to relax. In confronting someone who holds grudges, we must remind them of the truth of Ephesians 4:26, 27. We must also point out that God will deal with them as they deal with others (see Matthew 6:15; 18:21-35).

3. *Is it possible that the things that other people do that anger us the most may be the very things that we have problems with, too?* The teens will probably say yes to this question. There may be a couple of reasons why this is true: a) we see our own inconsistencies in others; b) since we are impatient with ourselves, we become impatient with others who reflect our inconsistencies.

CLOSING

Conclude this session by having teens divide into pairs. Ask them to share with their partner about one specific area in their life in which they are prone to get angry. Encourage them to take a few moments to pray for one another, asking God to give them the strength to control their anger and use it wisely.

SESSION 2

HOW TO HANDLE WORRY

OBJECTIVES

As a result of this session, teens should be able to do one or more of the following:

1. Define the word *worry*.
2. Identify the cause of worry.
3. Express four results of worry.
4. Turn over at least one specific thing they have been worried about to God.

ADVANCE PREPARATION

1. Make copies of Worksheet 3 and Transparencies B and C from the masters at the end of this unit.
2. Secure an overhead projector and screen to use with the transparency.
3. Be sure there are plenty of Bibles, paper, and pencils available for use.

MEETING SCHEDULE

Ready	5 minutes
Research	25 minutes
Respond	25 minutes
Closing	5 minutes

RESOURCE MATERIAL

A good definition of worry is *"a divided mind."* To be worried is to have your mind divided between two subjects or goals. To be worried is to be preoccupied with two things at the same time. It is impossible for a person to be totally effective at anything if his mind is divided, or if there is some internal conflict within him. A good illustration of this would be that of an athlete who is trying to perform in a key game when his father is sick in the hospital. His concern for his dad keeps him from concentrating on the big game. The Scripture passage for this

session deals with the issue of worry. In Matthew 6:25-34, Jesus basically asks the following question: *"How can you seek first God's will in your life if you're worried about clothes, food, and other external matters of this life?"* The answer is relatively simple. We can't put God first and worry at the same time. God has promised to give us that which we need. As a result, we can focus on doing His work in the world. Some people claim that worry is a part of their emotional make-up, and that they are unable to keep from worrying. But worry is not what some call a "neutral" emotion. It is negative. Worry prevents us from doing positive things for God's kingdom. When we fail to benefit God's kingdom we are actually benefiting the kingdom of Satan.

What do you do when things are uncertain in your life? What kind of life-style do you lead in general? Compare yourself with the following chart. What areas do you need to quit worrying about so you can concentrate more effectively on seeking God's kingdom?

Worry vs. Prayer

Worry produces:	Prayer produces:
insecurity	confidence
restlessness	peace of mind
poor witness	authentic Christianity
ulcers	good health
double vision	pure heart
fatigue	strength
lack of trust	total assurance
misplaced values	seeking first the kingdom of God

52

Young people worry about many things. Since they are halfway between childhood and adulthood, they do not yet know that most of the things they worry about will eventually work out. Some of the most powerful causes of worry among young people are their physical appearance, their grades, asking someone out or being asked to go out, getting into trouble with their parents, their career selections, etc.

It is unfortunate that many young people, even those who have grown up in Christian families, come from homes where their parents have modeled a life-style of worry. If this is true, it will be very difficult to *turn the tide* in one session. However, stress that there are two kinds of people in life: those who worry and those who pray. Those who never take their needs or worries to God in prayer will reap the results of worry. While many are tempted to worry when life is uncertain, those who pray are the ones who will receive the "peace of God, which surpasses all comprehension" (Philippians 4:7, *NASB).*

SESSiON PLaN

Ready

Project Transparency B on the screen for everyone to see. Read these statements aloud to the group and ask them to decide which one they feel is the most correct. Ask a few members of your group to explain why they chose what they did. Then ask them to list the statement they feel is most incorrect. It is not necessary for all the students to agree. This activity is merely designed to introduce this session on worry. Teens will hopefully be more aware of the correct answers when the session is over. Lead into the *Research* section by sharing the following thoughts.

"There's no person here who has not worried greatly about some thing or some person at one time or another. During this time together, we want to talk about worry and learn what

Jesus had to say about this subject. As a result of this session, we should be better equipped to control our tendency to worry?"

RESEARCH

Use one or more of the following activities to continue this session.

1. Worry: The Definition
To give the teens a proper definition for the subject of worry, ask them to look up Matthew 6:25-34 in their Bibles. Ask someone to read these verses to the rest of the group. After the passage is read, project Transparency C on the screen for everyone to see. Give a brief lecture (no more than 4-5 minutes) on the nature of worry. Use the *resource material* for this session to develop your thoughts.

2. Worry: It's Cause and Result
Share with teens that the basic cause of worry is misplaced values, which involves placing too great an emphasis on things of this world. When our focus is on the material things of life, it becomes easy to believe that these "things" equal life itself. Jesus said that life was more than food, drink, and clothing. What we value is what we worry about. To illustrate this point, divide teens into four groups. Each group should present a pantomime that will illustrate one of the ideas described below. A pantomime is a skit that uses only action to convey a message. There is to be no talking in this type of skit. The ideas given below are simply suggestions. If the students can think of a better skit that would illustrate the same result, encourage them to prepare and act it out.

Each of the following pantomimes show how misplaced values lead to a negative result.

Pantomime 1
This skit should demonstrate that one result of worry is nervousness and depression.

Depict a young person who is frantically studying for final exams. Show that his/her study is turning into a nervous frenzy because he/she is overly worried about getting a good grade.

Pantomime 2
This pantomime should illustrate that worry can lead us to doubt God.

Show a man trying to pay his bills. It is obvious that there is not enough money to cover all his expenses. Then show him turning to the

Bible for strength. He thumbs through the pages looking for answers, but finally becomes disgusted and tosses the Bible aside, still worried and doubting that God will be able to help him make ends meet.

Pantomime 3

This pantomime should explain how worry can result in physical illness.

Show a person standing in front of the mirror, obviously concerned about his/her appearance. The person is worried about getting every hair in place and making himself/herself look perfect. Then show the person on a date, still overly concerned about his/her appearance and unable to eat in the restaurant. Show him/her holding his/her stomach and finally looking sick. Show some people coming in, giving him/her assistance and carrying him/her off to the hospital.

Pantomime 4

This pantomime should demonstrate that worry leads to wasted time.

Show a parent waiting up late at night for a son or daughter to come in from a date. Show the parent trying to be busy and productive. However, he/she is unable to accomplish anything significant because of his/her worry.

After each pantomime has been acted out before the rest of the group, be sure to ask teens if they understood what was the result of worry in each skit.

Conclude this activity by explaining that even though worry is an emotion that we keep to ourselves, it will still be detrimental to our lives.

RESPOND

To help teens make the final application for this session on worry, distribute Worksheet 3. For each of the 3 situations, ask teens to match the appropriate Scripture *and* Life Principles to produce peace rather than worry. The correct answers are as follows: Situation 1—Philippians 4:6, Pray to God; Situation 2—Philippians 4:8, Focus your mind and thoughts on God; Situation 3—Matthew 6:34, Live one day at a time.

When teens have finished the exercise, be sure you answer any questions they may have. Then, as time allows, use as many of the following discussion questions as you wish. You may want to allow teens to discuss these in one large group or in several smaller groups.

DISCUSSION QUESTIONS

1. Jesus used logic and common sense in Matthew 6:25-34 to explain why there is no need to worry and why worry is useless. Which of the verses specifically express these ideas.
2. How does Jesus assure us we will be taken care of? How are we more valuable than birds and flowers? How can this help us overcome worry?
3. What do you think Jesus means when He tells us not to worry about such things as physical needs?
4. What does it mean to seek first God's kingdom? What promise is found in Matthew 6:33?
5. How can you begin to show that you believe this promise of Scripture?
6. What comes to mind when you hear, "Cast all your anxiety on him because he cares for you" (1 Peter 5:7, *NIV)?*
7. How is a disciplined thought life related to worry?
8. What is the difference between worry and concern?

CLOSING

To conclude this session, ask teens to think of one thing about which they have been worried recently. Give them approximately one minute to pray silently, confessing this worry to God and asking for strength to overcome it. Close with an audible prayer.

SESSION 3

HOW TO HANDLE INSECURITY

OBJECTIVES

As a result of this session, teens should be able to do one or more of the following:

1. Discover a Biblical basis for a good self-image.

2. Understand that a person's self-image can be influenced by certain factors.

3. Encourage someone else by naming a good quality he or she possesses.

ADVANCE PREPARATION

1. Prepare the 3 x 5 cards as instructed in the *Research* section for the *Mix and Match* activity.

2. Prepare any materials you wish to make available for the *Self-Image Development* activity in the *Respond* section.

3. Be sure there are plenty of Bibles, paper, and pencils available for use.

MEETING SCHEDULE	
Ready	10 minutes
Research	15 minutes
Respond	25 minutes
Closing	10 minutes

RESOURCE MATERIAL

Developing a proper self-image is one of the most important things one can do in life. Without it we feel insecure. What we imagine ourselves to be is one of the strongest motivators we have. Our imagination is often stronger than our will. If we can visualize ourselves as being or doing something, we can probably accomplish it.

In this session, teens will discover six principles for developing a good self-image. As the leader, you need to be familiar with these and be able to explain them in more detail if needed. Some thoughts are provided here for your personal study.

1. *God prescribed us before we were born.* This does not mean that God predetermined our physical characteristics, what our future careers might be, and whether or not we would make it to Heaven. It does mean that God made us human beings and said that it all was "very good" (see Genesis 1:26). Physical features such as eyes, lips, ears, teeth, skin complexion, etc., are mainly hereditary. They are determined by the genetic code of the parents. God made all human beings the same in the sense that they have the same general makeup (two eyes, two ears, two arms, two legs, etc.). Variations in the size of external features do not matter to God.

2. *God is not finished making us yet.* God *has finished* making us on the outside, but wants to *remake* our personalities and characters. He still wants to *work on us* in the person of His Spirit living within us. If God feels that we are important enough to want to live in us, then we must see ourselves as special. This allows us to accept our weaknesses, because we know that God is trying to improve them.

3. *The cause of inferiority is comparison with others.* Any type of comparison produces feelings of superiority or inferiority. Comparison with others is a very common occurrence among people today—particularly young peo- ple. This type of thinking is reinforced in every dimension of our lives. Class valedictorians are chosen on the basis of grade comparison. Miss America is chosen after she has been compared with others. Products are repeatedly compared on television. If our self-concepts are based on how well we rate in comparison to our neighbor, we'll always lose in the long run. By comparing ourselves with others, we will never have the proper view of self that God intended for us to have. This is the root cause of insecurity.

4. *Outward beauty is not essential to inward happiness.* One great lie Satan has succeeded in perpetrating is that physical attractiveness equals happiness. We live in a society that caters to the young and the beautiful. Those who have terminal cases of acne are often sloughed over. The popular people at school are usually the good looking ones. If this is true among youth groups, then the church is practicing Satan's directive, not God's. Are people accepted in your youth group on the basis of their physical attractiveness? If so, it reinforces the *world's* view of self-worth. If we believe that we are worth more because we look good, the devil has succeeded in deceiving us.

5. *God has an inward ideal He wants us all to reach.* This inward ideal is *His* character. Every person is to be like Christ. This is essential, not

COMPARING YOURSELF WITH OTHERS

optional. While we will all be at different levels in our spiritual maturity, we are all to aim toward Christlikeness. The more we become like Christ, the more we will like ourselves and the more secure we will feel. The more we become like Christ, the better we will be able to serve God in this world.

6. *Our self-worth is increased when we help others grow in Christ.* We live in an achievement-oriented society. But self-worth is not increased simply by accomplishing great things in the world. God is not concerned whether or not I earn a million dollars, am the school's top football player, or get straight "A's" in all my classes. God wants me to help others grow closer to Him. I experience worth, value, and security when others are brought closer to God because of me.

In his book, *Hide or Seek,* James Dobson says that the following things are the bases for a good self-image in today's society: beauty, brains, and money. Many Christian young people have bought this philosophy. Be ready to talk about this philosophy openly and candidly in this session. Be sure to stress that while it is not sinful to be rich, intelligent, or beautiful, the Bible does not say that these things are an adequate base for our self-image.

Most people base their feelings about themselves by how they think others view them. We need to focus upon what God thinks about us and base our self-images on that. The Bible says that God loves us. Once we can convince ourselves of that truth, we will have no reason to question our worth again.

SESSION PLAN

READY

Use one of the following activities to introduce this session.

1. What's in Your Wallet?
Ask teens to take out their wallets or billfolds. Have each person show and explain the cards in his wallet that have to do with his identity (who he is). Some examples might be a driver's license, a picture of his family, an ID from school, a social security card, etc. If your group is large, you may want to choose a few people to share some items from their wallets, instead of everybody doing it.

At the end of this activity, have teens discuss those things they learned about others that they did not know before they came. Then share the following thoughts with the group.

"The things we have just shared together have given us some idea of the identity of the people in this room. However, this information is inadequate to fully describe each person's identity. During this session, we are going to talk about handling insecurity. All of us have probably felt insecure at some time. Our feelings of insecurity are based in a poor self-image. The feelings we have about ourselves need to be based on more than the simple information we have shared. We should base our self-concepts on principles of Scripture rather than worldly values. That is the only way we can feel secure about ourselves."

2. How Do You Spend Your Time?
Give each young person a piece of paper and a pencil. Instruct the members of your group to draw a circle on their pieces of paper. The circle should represent the life of each one. Ask them to divide the circle on their papers into sections according to how much time they spend performing various activities. Have them label each of these sections and be ready to share their responses with the rest of the group. When everyone has had an opportunity to explain their circle with the group, share thoughts included in the previous activity.

RESEARCH

MIX AND MATCH

Copy each of the following statements and Scriptures on 3 x 5 cards. Distribute one card per teen, so that each group member will either have a statement or a Scripture. If you have fewer than twelve members in your group, you may give more than one piece of paper to each one. If you have more than 12 members, you may want to duplicate some sentences or Scriptures. (Note: if you duplicate one Scripture, be sure the statement corresponding to it is duplicated as well.)

Scriptures

Genesis 1:26
Ephesians 2:10; Philippians 2:12, 13
2 Corinthians 10:12
1 Samuel 16:7
Matthew 5:3-12
2 Corinthians 3:2; 1 Thessalonians 2:20

Statements

1. God prescribed us before we were born.
2. God is not finished making us yet.
3. The cause of inferiority is comparison with others.
4. Outward beauty is not essential to inward happiness.
5. God has an inward ideal He wants all of us to reach.
6. Self-worth is increased when we help others grow in Christ.

Tell the teens with the Scripture cards to look up their assigned passages. Then have everyone mingle together and try to match the correct statement with the correct Scripture.

After everyone has found his partner, have each person read his Scripture and/or statement to the group.

Share with the teens, "These Scriptures give us a Biblical basis for a good self-image. It is important that we base who we are on God's Word, and not on the ways of the world." If you wish to elaborate more on the subject, you may share any of the resource material that you think is pertinent. Emphasize that God gives a solid basis for a good self-image. The world doesn't.

RESPOND

SELF-IMAGE DEVELOPMENT

Divide teens into at least four groups of no more than four members each. Within these groups, they are to illustrate how one's self-image is influenced by given factors.

Assign one of the factors to each group. If you have more than four groups, allow more than one group to develop each factor.

Factor 1
One's self-image is affected by innate abilities and gifts (examples: high intelligence, good health, attractive appearance, skills, talents, economic status, etc.).

Factor 2
One's self-image is affected by positive feedback from those who are close to the person (example: parents, teachers, friends, brothers, sisters, etc.).

Factor 3
One's self-image is affected by comparing oneself or being compared to others.

Factor 4
One's self-image is affected by dwelling on past failures and defeats.

Once you have assigned the above factors, allow teens to illustrate the concept in whichever way they choose. Some ways teens may illustrate their factors are as follows.

1. Make a montage from magazine pictures and lettering (a montage is a grouping of words and pictures to illustrate one concept).
2. Draw a cartoon on a transparency or a large piece of poster paper.
3. Act out a commercial.
4. Make a bumper sticker.

Be sure to have the necessary materials available which are needed to complete these activities.

After each group has finished developing their activity, allow them to share their *production* with the rest of the group.

When all the groups have had the opportunity to make their presentations, share the following thoughts with the entire group.

"These factors that were just illustrated can be positive and help enhance our self-images. However, they can affect us negatively and make us feel insecure as well. This problem arises when we try to base our security on these external factors. These factors in the proper perspective can help us build and maintain a good self-concept; but the true basis for our very existence must always be God and His Word."

DISCUSSION QUESTIONS

Have your teens arrange their chairs in a circle. Lead them into a discussion time by using the questions listed below. As they share, lead them to apply the truths of this session to their lives.

1. "Sticks and stones may break my bones, but words will never hurt me." Do you agree or disagree with this statement? Why? Give an example of a time when words hurt deeply.
2. How can we keep from comparing ourselves with others?
3. How can knowing Christ help a person improve his self-image?
4. Share a time when some external thing was taken from you and you felt it hurt your self-image. (Example: You are a football player, and you base much of your self-concept on the fact that you are an athlete. However, you broke your leg recently and are going to miss out on an entire season.)
5. Suppose we began accepting people into our youth group or class on the basis of worldly standards, i.e. popularity, looks, status, talents, etc. How could such an action be detrimental to our unity? How can we avoid this?

CLOSING

Go around the circle and ask each teen to name one good quality about the person on his right. Ask them to be as specific and honest as possible. Close in prayer, thanking God for each person in the group.

session 4

HOW TO HANDLE GUILT

OBJECTIVES

As a result of this session, teens should be able to do one or more of the following:
1. Identify what makes people feel guilty.
2. Discover two ways to handle guilt.
3. Discern the proper way to handle guilt and to become free of it.

ADVANCE PREPARATION

1. Make copies of Worksheet 4 and Transparencies D and E from the masters at the end of this unit.

2. If you use the *Name That Person* activity in the *Research* section, you will need to contact five young people to prepare testimonies prior to the session. Further details are given in the session plan.

3. Be sure there are plenty of Bibles, paper, and pencils available for use.

MEETING SCHEDULE	
Ready	10 minutes
Research	20 minutes
Respond	20 minutes
Closing	10 minutes

RESOURCE MATERIAL

Guilt is one of the strongest emotions in life. Young people who suffer from guilt need help. This session deals with the principles your young people need to overcome feelings of guilt in their lives.

This final session examines the sin of David and Bathsheba. Read 2 Samuel 11:1-27 several times so that you are very familiar with the entire story. Be sure that you have the events of the story in chronological order. They are listed below for your convenience.

1. David saw Bathsheba bathing.
2. David called for her, and they committed adultery.
3. Bathsheba became pregnant.
4. David sent for Uriah, Bathsheba's husband, in an effort to cover up his sin.
5. Uriah slept outside the palace and did not go into his own house.
6. David got Uriah drunk, hoping that then he would go home.
7. Uriah again slept with his master's servants and did not go home.
8. David sent a letter to Joab commanding that Uriah be put in the front line of the next battle.
9. Uriah was killed.
10. David took Bathsheba to be his wife.

It is important to realize that David wanted to get Uriah home because Bathsheba was pregnant. If people knew Uriah was home about the time Bathsheba became pregnant, they would suspect Uriah, not David, to be the father of the child. When that scheme did not work, David then conspired to have Uriah murdered by sending him to the front lines of battle.

In Psalm 32, David contrasts the way both he and God dealt with the guilt experienced as a result of David's sin with Bathsheba. David thought that if he kept his guilt inside of him and didn't talk about it, it would eventually go away. David's solution to overcoming guilt was wrong. The only way David was able to eliminate his guilt was to fully confess it to God. Only then did David receive the joy and forgiveness he desired so much.

GUILT IN YOUNG PEOPLE

Very few young people understand what it means to be maturing in Christ. As a result, many Christian teens suffer from a tremendous amount of guilt. This session should emphasize the security we have in Christ, and the freedom we can have from guilt (assuming your teens are already Christians).

Keep in mind that some young people will suffer from a type of general guilt simply because they accepted Christ and were baptized at a very young age. Now that they are in their teenage years, they begin to understand more fully what it means to have Jesus as the Lord of their lives. As a result, they become acutely aware of the number of years in which they "did nothing" for Jesus. This produces a type of spiritual agony that this session can help them overcome.

Some young people feel guilty because they can remember so vividly the sins they have committed in the past. They reason, "If *I* can remember my past sins, then surely God remembers my sins. After all, He probably has a better memory than I do." Such reasoning is not true. The Bible clearly states that God forgets the sins of a repentant person (see Hebrews 10:17). In Christ, we are forgiven. We will receive no condemnation.

Another reason why young people might feel guilty is that they live around people who remind them of their past sins. No one likes to be reminded of past wrongdoings. The body of Christ can be either a source or therapy or a thorn in the flesh when it comes to dealing with guilt. If God has forgotten our mistakes, the church must also forget the mistakes of others.

Session Plan

Ready

Choose one of the following activities to begin this session.

1. Thinking Back

Ask teens to think back to when they were younger. Encourage them to share a time when they did something they knew was wrong, but when confronted about their actions, they made up an excuse to rationalize their wrongdoing. (In order for this activity not to be threatening, encourage your young people to share an experience they can laugh about now). If you have a small group, encourage everyone to share. If you have a large group, you might divide them up into pairs and allow them to share with each other. Then call on a few to share with the large group. Then share the following thoughts.

"The final session of this study deals with one of the most troubling emotions know to man: guilt. Some modern psychologists have said that there is no such things as true guilt. There is, they say, a false guilt, based on what people have conditioned us to believe is right or wrong.

"The Bible openly discusses both sin and guilt. Guilt is a natural consequence of sin. But guilt does not have to stifle our energies forever. God intended us to deal with our guilt and experience His forgiveness."

2. Conscience Wheel

Begin this session by asking some of your students to define the word, "conscience." After several comments, explain that the Indians had an interesting way of describing one's conscience. (Draw the diagram illustrated here on a chalkboard or a large piece of newsprint.)

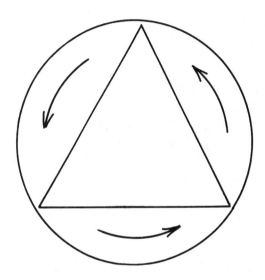

The Indians believed that one's conscience was like a sharp-edged triangle that spun around in the center of one's mind. They thought that if someone did something wrong, the outer edges of his brain would move in on the triangle so that the corners of the triangle pricked his mind. This painful pricking is referred to today as a "guilty conscience." The Indians further believed if a person continued to violate his conscience, the corners of the triangle would eventually break off, and he would lose any sense of conscience whatsoever. The Bible refers to this condition as a "seared conscience" (see 1 Timothy 4:2).

Ask teens if they think this analogy the Indians used was a good one. Ask them to give reasons why they agree or disagree with the analogy.

Lead into this session by sharing the same thoughts that were given for the previous *Ready* activity.

RESEARCH

DaviD anD BaTHSHeBa

Ask teens to recall as many facts as they can about the story of David and Bathsheba. Be prepared to do the following things as group members share:

1. Praise any proper statements made by your students;
2. Correct any statements that do not properly correspond to the story; and
3. Place all your students' remarks in correct chronological order.

For information regarding this story, read 2 Samuel 11 and 12, as well as the resource material provided for this session. As you finish sharing, point out that David suffered a lot of guilt as a result of his sin with Bathsheba.

Two ways To HanDle GuilT

Give teens the opportunity at this time to read Psalm 32:1-11. If you have enough Bibles, allow them to individually read the passage from their Bibles. If you would rather try a different approach to the reading of Scripture, here's an idea: copy the words of the Psalm on a large piece of newsprint or on an overhead transparency. Display the material before the group at the appropriate time, and do one of three things:

1. Read the passage of Scripture aloud to them,
2. Have two or three teens read the passage aloud, while the rest of the group follows along, or
3. Read the passage of Scripture responsively.

When you have finished reading, ask teens to locate the wrong approach to guilt that David

first used. This is found in verses 3 and 4. Then ask them to locate the correct approach to guilt that David used. This is found in verses 5 through 7 of Psalm 32.

As teens look up the two ways to handle guilt, prepare to display Transparency D. As you share the information on the transparency, be sure they understand both ways David tried to handle his guilt. Be sure to include the method and the ultimate result for each one. Point out to your students that many people try to use David's first approach in overcoming guilt. Naturally, such action does not bring the desired result. For additional comments, refer to the resource material provided for this session.

Name THaT PerSon

If you choose to do this activity you will need to notify the people involved at least one week in advance. Ask five teens to portray Bible characters who experienced guilt. The five Bible characters (four skits) are:

1. Adam *and* Eve (Genesis 3:6-13)
2. the prodigal son (Luke 15:11-21)
3. Judas (Matthew 26:47-49; 27:3-5)
4. Peter (Matthew 26:69-75; John 21:15-19).

Each participant should prepare a two-minute testimony explaining the sin of the person they are portraying. Within the testimony, the teens need to explain how their assigned Bible characters reacted to the guilt they experienced as a result of their sin. Instruct the *actors* not to give the name of the character they are portraying. It will be up to the group to guess their identity.

When the actors have finished giving their *testimonies,* ask the rest of the group to determine which of the characters had the right response and which had the wrong. You may want to share the following thoughts with the group.

"Adam and Eve played the *Blame Game.* Adam blamed Eve for his sin; and Eve blamed the serpent. Neither wanted to admit that they were responsibile for their own sin. We often act the same.

"Judas' reaction to his guilt was one of total despair. He must have thought that Jesus never would have forgiven him, and so he simply took his life. Many of us have done some crazy things when we thought that the forgiveness of God was unattainable.

"The prodigal son and Peter had the right idea. Their sorrow lead to repentance and confession which freed them from guilt."

RESPOND

HOW TO BE FREE FROM GUILT

Share with the group that David provides us with some practical steps toward being free from guilt. Use the following thoughts to help them understand this concept.

"There are three steps to being free from guilt that are found in verses 8-11 of Psalm 32.

"Verse 8 speaks of the first step to removing guilt—*listen to God's instruction and counseling.* This is God's instruction to us. When we study His Word, we develop a godly conscience within us. In order to be free from and prevent guilt, we must *listen* to God's instruction and counsel. David said, "Thy word I have treasured in my heart, that I may not sin against Thee" (Psalm 119:11, NASB). The person who *listens* to God's counsel will think like Him, and protect himself from sin.

"The second step to being free from guilt is *obedience.* In Psalm 32:9 David says, "Do not be as the horse or as the mule which have no understanding" (NASB). David pictures the concept of stubbornness. Some animals must have bits put in their mouths and bridles around their necks so that their master can *jerk* them in the direction he wants them to go. We are not to be like that. Our response to our Master is to be one of cooperation. When we cooperate with God by *obeying* His Word, we have taken a big step toward being free from guilt from our lives. David resisted admitting his guilt for nearly a year from the time he committed adultery with Bathsheba. He was like a stubborn, rebellious mule who wasn't going to submit to his master. Because of this experience, David concluded that it was best to *obey* God and cooperate with Him.

"The third and final step to being free from guilt that David explains in Psalm 32 is *trust*. David says, "He who *trusts* in the Lord, loving-kindness shall surround him" (Psalm 32:10, NASB). We must *trust* God, not our feelings. If we believe we're forgiven only when we *feel* forgiven, many of us will be in big trouble. If God says we are forgiven, then we are forgiven! That settles it! Our responsibility is to trust God at His word. There can be nothing more deceiving than trusting our feelings.

"When we listen to God's counsel, obey His commands, and trust His promises, we are beginning to be free from today's guilt and prevent tomorrow's problems."

DISCUSSION QUESTIONS

Distribute Worksheet 4. Guide the group in a discussion of these steps to being free from guilt by using the discussion questions on the worksheet. As the discussion progresses, use any material you feel is pertinent from the resource material. The questions are listed here for your convenience.

1. What consequences have you seen when a person does not attempt to remove his guilt?

2. How does a person receive counsel from the Lord?
3. How long does it take to develop a godly conscience?
4. How long does it take to lose your conscience?
5. What are some things that a person might have to do to remove his guilt?
6. What happens if a person remains stubborn and is unwilling to cooperate with God?
7. Have you ever seen this kind of stubbornness in real life? Describe the situation without describing the people involved.
8. How do feelings keep us from forgetting our past mistakes?
9. Why can't feelings be trusted?

CLOSING

Project Transparency E on the screen so that everyone can see it. Explain to the group that this drawing vividly illustrates the way God does not see our sin through Christ. As Christians, Jesus' sacrificial death has removed our guilt and freed us to serve God. Refer to the resource material for any additional thoughts you may want to share.

In closing, have a special prayer time encouraging teens to use the three steps shared in this session in dealing with any unresolved feelings of guilt.

ePHesians 4:26,27

"Be angry, and yet do not sin; do not let the sun go down on your anger, and do not give the devil an opportunity" (NASB).

"'In your anger do not sin': Do not let the sun go down while you are still angry, and do not give the devil a foothold" *(NIV)*.

DiscUSSiON QUeSTiONS

1. What steps could a person take to overcome his anger?

2. How could you confront a person who is quick to get angry or prone to hold grudges?

3. Is it possible that the things that other people do that anger us the most may be the very things that we have problems with, too?

Match these four causes of anger with the appropriate cartoon: 1) selfishness, 2) frustration, 3) injustice, 4) pain.

Permission to reproduce individual worksheets granted.

CURE FOR WORRY

Match each situation with the appropriate Scripture and life principle.

Situation	Scripture	Life Principle
1. Mr. Jones talks to his family about the possibility of him changing jobs, and the whole family moving with him to another state. His son, Bob, however, had hoped to complete his high school education where the family lives now. With his father considering this new job, Bob is worried that he may not be able to do as he would like. Bob doesn't know what else to do other than to seek God in prayer.	Matthew 6:34	Focus your mind and thoughts on God.
2. John is new at school. Since he is only 5 feet tall, he has been made fun of by some of the bigger guys. Some have actually threatened him with physical harm. As a result, John has been worried about being beaten up—so much so that he has been unable to sleep at night. Recently, however, John decided that the only thing he could do was to concentrate with his whole mind on God instead of the problem.	Philippians 4:6	Live one day at a time.
3. Mary just overheard her parents having a terrible fight. She fears they are about to get a divorce. She is not only worried for herself, but for her two younger brothers as well. She doesn't want the family to split up. Finally Mary realizes that this is too big for her to handle; worrying about it is not going to solve anything. She decides to live one day at a time.	Philippians 4:8	Pray to God

DISCUSSION QUESTIONS

Consider the following questions as you strive to apply the truths of today's lesson to your life.

1. What consequences have you seen in the person who does not attempt to remove guilt from his life?

2. How does a person receive counsel from the Lord?

3. How long does it take to develop a godly conscience?

4. How long does it take for a person to lose his conscience?

5. What are some things a person may have to do to remove his guilt?

6. What happens if a person remains stubborn and unwilling to cooperate with God?

7. Have you ever seen this kind of stubbornness in real life? Describe the situation without mentioning names.

8. How do feelings keep us from forgetting our past mistakes?

9. Why can't feelings be trusted.

WHaT Can We DO aBOUT anGeR?

Permission to reproduce individual transparencies granted.

WORRY:
a DiViDED MiND

2 approaches to guilt

David   God

METHOD	
KEEP SILENT ABOUT IT	ACKNOWLEDGE GUILT (v.5)
HIDE IT	CONFESS IT (v.5)
RESULT	
BONES WASTED (v.3)	JOY (v.10)
GROANING (v.3)	
HAND WAS HEAVY UPON ME (v.4)	FORGIVENESS (v.5)
STRENGTH DRIED UP (v.4)	DELIVERANCE (v.7)

Behind the Scenes: Evaluating TV and Movies

BY JIM EICHENBERGER

INTRODUCTION

"Lights! Camera!! Action!!!"

Scientists, hoping to enrich the lives of people by giving them more access to information, literature, and art, invent an electronic box with a glowing screen. This box is designed to show moving pictures to people as they sit in the comfort of their own homes. The educational possibilities are endless! News events, cultural happenings, and many other interesting and even enriching activities can now be brought to the common man. The inventors are ecstatic!

But the beast turns upon its creators! The flashing pictures mesmerize their audience. People who used to go out and spend time socializing with friends now sit glued before a screen. Families who used to discuss the events of the day now "S-h-h-h" each other, straining eyes and ears in an effort not to miss a moment of what the magic box can offer viewers. In some homes the tube is never silent, invading meal times and hypnotizing viewers into the wee morning hours. Through the tube, characters come into homes which viewers would normally never allow through the door. Language and situations once deemed inappropriate for children to hear or see are delivered to young minds while mother and father allow the machine to baby-sit. The fiendish beast has seemingly conquered the world!

If this scenario were written fifty years ago, it would sound like a science fiction horror story. Unfortunately, this story is not fictional and is hardly exaggerated. The great panacea of television has turned into slavery for many people. And with the advent of new technology, the problem shows no signs of lessening. Cable television, combined with videotape and video disk technologies, have blurred the distinctions between television and movies (the rationale for grouping them together in this unit). Technological capabilities have opened the media floodgates, allowing easy access to questionable and even pornographic material to all people, regardless of age.

The growth of the media industry is virtually unchecked. Yet, so many questions as to the media's effects are still left unanswered. Educators are now wondering if viewing actually changes the way that youngsters learn. Social scientists attempt to discover links between the anti-social behavior of young viewers and the types of programming they watch. With so many questions still unanswered, the monster of the electronic media continues to grow.

This unit is an approach to help teens use Scriptural principles to evaluate and control personal viewing habits. Here is the outline of the development of this study.

Session One, *TV and Movies . . . and Your Time,"* examines viewing habits in light of Paul's admonition to "redeem the time." Does watching TV waste time, or does it also pose dangers to the constructive use of non-viewing hours?

Session Two, *"TV and Movies . . . and Your Relationships,"* compares the Biblical models of male/female relationships, family relationships, and employer/employee relationships to the Hollywood counterparts. Which model are teenagers more likely to follow?

Session Three, *"TV and Movies . . . and Your Mind,"* confronts the issue of world-view. How does the mind of God view faith, man, and sin as compared to the mind of the screen? How is a teen's world-view being shaped by subtle (and not-so-subtle) video programming?

Finally, **Session Four,** *"TV and Movies . . . and Your Choices,"* ties the entire package together. When teens correlate what has been learned, they need to decide how to make decisions regarding viewing habits and glorify God.

The question of TV and movies is too often met by the church with either ire or apathy. This unit is designed to bring Biblical principles to focus upon this great challenge facing our youth. May we succeed in so *broadcasting* the message of the Savior!

Service Project Christian Home Entertainment Guide

While the topic of evaluating television and movies is an appropriate subject for teens, it would be terribly shortsighted to believe that this topic is relevant to no one else. Christian adults, especially young adults who have grown up in the TV age and are now parents, need to be challenged concerning their entertainment choices.

Teenagers in your youth group could provide a great service to the congregation by publishing a guide to Christian home entertainment. The guide could be published just once, as a project in conjunction with this unit. But a guide could be even more effective as an ongoing weekly, monthly, or quarterly publication.

An innovative group of teens will be able to create a nearly endless supply of ideas for the guide. Since the guide will probably be no larger than one sheet of paper (typed on the front and back), different features could appear from issue to issue. Here are some content ideas to consider.

1. **Feature Articles**
   The entertainment industry makes news in our country. The reporters in charge of feature stories need to read newspapers and newsmagazines to be aware of important developments. What does the growth in cable networks mean for Christians? Do recent surveys of the effects of TV violence support a Biblical view of man's sinful nature? What can Christians do about pornographic films? Questions such as these could make for thought-provoking articles for both teens and adults.

2. **TV Series Review/Recommended Movie**
   A review of a movie or TV program from a

Christian viewpoint could be a valuable feature for the entertainment guide.

3. "Now Playing" Digest

Some magazines used to provide a numeral or star rating for currently playing films, based upon the review of a few different periodicals. Teens could scan newspapers and magazines to develop a similar capsule review. Perhaps a review of five or ten movies playing in local theatres would be helpful to readers of the guide.

4. Testimonies

It would be helpful to include suggestions from families who have successfully controlled their viewing habits. Suggestions on how to gain control of the tube and testimonies as to the results of this feat would both be appropriate.

Once the youth group gets excited about this project, you will need to organize the effort. There is plenty of work for *everyone* in the group! Here are some suggested committees.

Editorial Staff

As mentioned before, not everything will fit on two sides of paper. Someone has to decide what content will be used in each issue. After deciding what is needed, this staff should see that the work is assigned, and that material submitted for publication is the proper style and length.

Reporters

Reporters are necessary to research and write the feature articles and reviews. While teens who are leader types often made good editors, the quiet "bookworms" would be exemplary reporters.

Production

Who will type the articles? Will the guide be run on a ditto machine, mimeograph, photocopier, or offset press? Will paste-up be necessary? Teens with office skills will be useful on this staff.

Circulation

The guide may be mailed along with the church newsletter on a regular basis. Perhaps distribution to the Sunday school classes is best for your situation. Maybe stuffing the guides inside the church bulletin would be better yet. Regardless of how the publication is circulated, members of the youth group will have to do it.

A Christian home entertainment guide could be an exciting project, not just for your group but for the entire church. Both teen and adult church members, as Christians, need to tackle the challenge of evaluating the entertainment media.

POSSiBLE CiRCULATiON MeTHOD

SOCial activity SaTURDAY Night aT THe movies

A natural complement to this unit's educational activities is a Movie Night Social. Here are a few ideas you can use.

1. Movie Night

Plan a *Movie Night* event for the entire group. Make sure to have plenty of popcorn and soft drinks to serve during the film.

While there are numerous movies that could be shown on a night like this, it would be wise to choose a film that would help reinforce the message of this series of sessions. At the writing of this book, Life Productions has just released a new movie called, *They Lied to Us.* This is a film "that explores the lives of several young people who 'bought the lies' of TV, magazines, music, movies, and their friends . . . and suffered the consequences." The intent of the movie is to show young people how they can make a distinction between God's truth and the lie's of the world that are propagated through the media. The viewing of this film could be followed by a very productive discussion. You will want to plan this activity about the same time as you plan to use Session 3 because this film would fit in particularly well with its content.

This movie is 45 minutes long and rents for $66 plus shipping and handling. It may be available through your local Christian film distributor or contact:

Life Productions
1655 Peachtree Street
Suite 1114
Atlanta, GA 30309
(404)/892-3213

2. Teen Created Entertainment

While this approach can be time-consuming, the rewards are well worth the effort. Teens may write, act, and produce their own films or movies via the medium of movie/video camera. Perhaps a live performance could be presented to a senior citizens' home. This performance could be videotaped, and then shown during the Movie Night. Whenever possible, encourage teens to create scenes and produce material. Involvement does pay off! Make this a fun event that will entice non-Christian teens. Create new opportunities for outreach.

Decide which approach is best—then start creating an atmosphere. Enlist teens' help in decorating for a "cinema look." Make posters, create a movie marquee, and construct a refreshment bar. Need a suggested menu? How about hot dogs, ice cream bars, soft drinks, and popcorn (of course). Be creative with arrangements!

RECOMMENDED RESOURCES

The Media Action Research Center in Los Angeles, CA is an independent, non-profit organization that researches the impact of television on viewers. They also create educational resources about the media's influence on society. One of their publications that you may find helpful is called *Media & Values.* This is a periodical that is published quarterly in cooperation with many church groups that are concerned with the effect of the media on those who are exposed to it. Annual subscriptions are available in the United States ($12), Canada ($14), and all others ($18). You may write for more information to the following address:

Media Action Research Center
1962 South Shenandoah
Los Angeles, CA 90034

Here are some other resources that you may find helpful as you prepare for these sessions. You may also want to make your group members aware of these resources for their personal study.

Frost, Marie. *Listen to Your Children.* Cincinnati: Standard Publishing, 1980. Chapter 14 (pp. 89-93) deals specifically with establishing correct priorities for TV viewing.

Liebert, Robert; Neale, John; and Davidson, Emily. *The Early Window.* Elmsford, New York: Pergamon Press, Inc., 1973. A concise summary of the *Surgeon General's Report on Television And Social Behavior,* this book helps to clarify research findings on the effects of television watching on behavior.

McCoy, Elin. "What TV Is Doing to Your Kids." *Parents,* June, 1981, pp. 54-60. This article examines the influence of television on children.

Winn, Marie. *The Plug-in Drug.* New York: Viking Press, 1977. An easy-to-read analysis of media addiction, this book provides practical help for breaking the TV habit.

session 1

TV, Movies, and... Your Time

advance preparation

1. Make copies of Worksheets 1 and 2, and Transparency A from the masters at the end of this unit.

2. Secure an overhead projector, screen, and marking pen.

3. If you choose the first *Ready* activity, you will need to bake a large cookie, about 9″ in diameter. A soft sugar cookie recipe, baked in a round cake pan, would be suitable. Also, bring a knife. This cookie will be sliced into very thin wedges during the session. You will also need a pocket calculator.

4. If you choose the second *Ready* activity, you will need to secure the album *Snooze, Ya Lose* by Isaac Air Freight. You will need a record player or cassette tape player to play the sketch called "Time Wasters Looks at TV."

5. Secure the album *So You Wanna Go Back to Egypt?* by Keith Green for use in the *Respond* section. You will need a record player or cassette tape player to play the song called "You Love the World and You're Avoiding Me!"

6. Bring poster paper, felt-tip pens, and copies of movie advertisements for the poster making activity.

7. Be sure to have plenty of Bibles, paper, and pencils available for use.

objectives

As a result of this session, teens should be able to do one or more of the following:

1. Recognize that they may spend much more time viewing TV and movies than in building their relationship with God.

2. List the priorities the Word of God has placed upon our time.

3. Describe some negative effects of excessive video viewing.

4. Attempt to schedule at least one positive non-media activity into their lives for the next week.

meeting schedule

Ready	10 minutes
Research	15 minutes
Respond	25 minutes
Closing	10 minutes

RESOURCE MATERIAL

How did we ever get along without it? The poor, unenlightened creatures of barely thirty years ago knew little of the magic box that plays such a central role in our society today. How did people ever survive?

It seems that most Americans cannot survive without television today. Even a cursory glance at contemporary life-styles illustrates that fact. Only the most inept home decorator would ever consider placing the most comfortable chair in the living room out of direct line with the glowing screen. Housewives plan their laundry, cooking, and cleaning chores around the "soaps." Sanitation experts in large cities know when commercial breaks in popular programs occur by the increased flow in flush water. And may Heaven help those church events unwisely scheduled to coincide with the telecasting of the Super Bowl or a World Series Game!

The well-educated mock the shallow plots and weak story lines of the bulk of televised fare. But, intellectuals watch. Critics call television a "wasteland." But, critics also watch. Even as Christians we decry the valueless society depicted on TV and are very uncomfortable with the medium's pre-occupation with sex and violence. *But, most Christians also watch TV.*

The content of TV and movies is a serious matter and will be discussed later. However, no matter what show is being watched, viewing takes time. And because scheduling is done by the broadcasters and not by us, TV often controls our use of time. The subject of the use of our time, therefore, is square one when discussing television's control on our individual lives.

When instructing Christians on how to conduct themselves as *"children of the light,"* the apostle Paul deals with the Christian's stewardship of his time: *"See then that ye walk circumspectly, not as fools, but as wise, redeeming the time, because the days are evil"* (Ephesians 5:15-16).

In calling us to budget properly the spending of our time, Paul lists four priorities for the Christian. A person who truly redeems the time will find himself occupied with these priorities.

1. Understanding God's Will

"Wherefore be ye not unwise, but understanding what the will of the Lord is" (Ephesians 5:17). A constant refrain in Jesus' earthly ministry was the assertion that He came to do the will of the One Who sent Him. Paul listed understanding God's will first among priorities for redeeming the time.

According to Paul, the *"mystery of his will"* has been revealed to us in Christ (Ephesians 1:9). God's will is not something we must seek to unlock by watching the movement of the stars, counting and tracing the lines in our palms, or analyzing dregs at the bottom of teacups. Neither is God's will something we will blindly happen upon, whether we seek it or not. We must be *"filled with the knowledge of his will in all wisdom and spiritual understanding"* (Colossians 1:9). A capped bottle cannot be filled. Likewise, we must open ourselves and desire to be filled with the knowledge of His will.

Of course, study of Scripture is the primary way to gain this knowledge. Also worthy of some of our time is the reading of Bible study aids, Christian books and magazines, and listening to Christian music.

But what happens to this priority when we are glued to the tube? Probably, we are just wasting time which could be used for better purposes. But there is still another danger. If we do not fill ourselves with the knowledge of God's will, we do not remain empty, in a vacuum. Paul indicates that we will fill ourselves with foolishness. We *do learn something* when we are immersed in the media. However, *what* we learn may simply quicken our own destruction.

2. Being Filled With the Spirit

"And be not drunk with wine, wherein is excess; but be filled with the Spirit" (Ephesians 5:18). In this second priority is the perfect complement to the first. We are to understand the will of God and then we are to be filled with His Spirit so that we may do His will.

As with understanding God's will, being filled with the Spirit is neither mystical nor automatic. God does not hide this power from us, but neither does He force it upon us.

The indwelling Spirit is a gift of God given to all Christians when they accept Christ as Savior (Acts 2:38; 19:2; Ephesians 1:13-14). Being filled with the Spirit, as used here, can possibly be best interpreted as an ongoing, day-to-day experience, rather than a one time event. Understood in this light, it would be a very similar phrase to *"Walk in the Spirit"* (Galatians 5:16) and *"to be strengthened with might by his Spirit"* (Ephesians 3:16). Although as Christians we do not have to go searching for His power (for He lives within us), God will not automatically strengthen and guide us against our will. The more we seek to walk with the Spirit, especially through prayer and Bible study, the more we will be filled and strengthened to do His will.

Obviously, developing this priority takes time—time, once again, which is often wasted in passive viewing rather than in active communion with the Father. Paul warns us not to be drunk with wine. How many Christians do not touch alcoholic beverages but are videoholics and are equally numbed to the Spirit? The *electronic tranquilizer,* like alcohol and other drugs, can weaken our defenses against temptation. At the same time, TV can take the place of the only power capable of winning the fight.

3. Worship and Fellowship

"Speaking to yourselves in psalms and hymns and spiritual songs, singing and making melody in your heart to the Lord" (Ephesians 5:19) illustrates the third priority for our time. Time management must recognize that humans are social creatures. Christianity is not "just me and Jesus." John described the results of walking *"in the light"* as two-fold—cleansing from sin and fellowship with one another *(1 John 1:7).* We are never to believe that meeting together for mutual encouragement, as well as for worship, is unimportant (Hebrews 10:24-25). In fact, we are continually to *"encourage one another and build each other up"* (1 Thessalonians 5:11, *NIV).* Whether working, playing, serving, or praying, we must invest time in each other.

Consider another disadvantage of movies and TV. Most people can put down a book to talk to someone who enters the room. We can begin that interrupted paragraph exactly where we left it. But not so with video and cinema. The flashing pictures never stop. The screen demands our full attention. If we are to derive full benefit of program content, human beings may have to take a back seat. Excessive TV viewing not only takes time from what we need to be doing, it also works against God's calling for the wise use of our time.

4. Thanksgiving

"Giving thanks always for all things unto God and the Father in the name of our Lord Jesus Christ" (Ephesians 5:20) exemplifies the fourth priority. To redeem the time, we are to spend it in 1) understanding God's will, 2) growing in our submission to the Spirit, 3) fulfilling God's will in our relationships with our fellow believers, and 4) wrapping the entire package in a spirit of thanksgiving and contentment.

It is disconcerting to see teenagers who are rich in material possessions but are obviously unhappy. A person may wonder if time spent watching TV may not add to this discontentment.

A quick census of the TV characters who populate Hollywood's fantasyland is revealing. Doctors, lawyers, oil tycoons, and other business "wheels" dominate the soaps. The average businessman and working woman on situation comedies dress as fashion models. TV characters often live in southern California-style condominiums. Add to this scene the constant barrage of advertising designed to push products leading to "true fulfillment"—even the most well-to-do viewer may wonder what is missing in his own life-style.

Notice that this session's primary concern is not what is on TV, but the fact that *the TV is on.* Not all television programs, however, are harmful. Indeed, there are many worthwhile TV shows. Viewers can learn much about life by watching educational and documentary programming. But regardless of its relative value, TV can waste time if not managed properly.

SESSION PLAN
READY

Use one of the following activities to begin this session.

1. How Do You Spend Your Time?

Distribute Worksheet 1 to teens. Give them a

few minutes to estimate the time spent in the past week on the following activities:

a. School attendance/Homework
b. Hobbies/Sports
c. Social functions
d. Bible reading/Prayer/Church
e. TV/Movies
f. Work (at home or job)
g. Other

(Note: Categories a-g should not include more than 100 hours per week. This assumes that teens get 9-10 hours of sleep per night. If the sum of categories a-g is greater than 100 hours, the student either made poor estimates or needs more sleep!)

Category by category, young people should call out their time estimates to a selected teen. This person will then total and average the time categories on a pocket calculator (Average equals the sum of times for a particular category divided by the number of teens). At the same time, record the averages on transparency A and fill in the *pie graph*.

Project the completed graph. Note the results, especially the slices for TV/Movies and for Prayer/Bible Reading/Church. If the teens in your group are average, TV/Movies will rate between 35-55 hours, while Bible reading and prayer will total between 2-5 hours. Cut a very small slice of cookie for each person (representing the slice in the graph designated for Bible reading, prayer, and church).

Then say the following: "How many of you are satisfied with the size of your cookie portion? In this session, we will discuss God's satisfaction with the *slice* of our lives we give to Him compared to the amount of time we spend on our own entertainment."

2. Time Wasters

There is an excellent Christian comedy group called Isaac Air Freight that puts out some humorous yet thought provoking sketches. There is a sketch called "Time Wasters Looks at TV" on the album *Snooze, Ya Lose* that deals with the way people waste their time by watching too much TV. If you choose this activity, play the sketch and then share the following thoughts with the group.

"This sketch helps us laugh at a situation that in reality is not very funny for many people. We have heard in a rather exaggerated way how some people are completely controlled by the tube. They waste hour after hour each day in front of the screen. Did you see a little bit of yourself in Harold? He was so intent on watching the TV that he almost completely ignored his visitor! Has that ever happened to you? How did it feel?

"We would all probably agree that we do not appreciate being treated like that. However, how does God feel when He sees the amount of time we willingly spend in front of the tube in comparison to the time we spend with Him? In this session, we want to consider this question and honestly appraise the use of our time so that it will not be wasted."

RESEARCH

SCRIPTURE SEARCH

Ask one member of the group to read Ephesians 5:15-16 aloud. Comment that the phrase *"redeeming the time"* is a key concern in this passage. Allow teens ten minutes to complete

Scripture Search Chart		
Scripture	Activity Commanded	How Does Excessive TV/Movie Viewing Hinder?
Ephesians 5:17 Colossians 1:9 Ephesians 1:9	Takes Time From Bible Study Understanding The Will of the Lord	Often Presents False Values
Ephesians 5:18 Galatians 5:16 Ephesians 3:16	Be Filled With (Walk in and Be Strengthened By) the Spirit	Takes Time From Prayer Temptation From Worldly Values
Ephesians 5:19 Colossians 3:16 Hebrews 10:24-25 1 Thessalonians 5:11	Worship & Fellowship	Isolates Viewer From Others Around Him
Ephesians 5:20 Colossians 3:17	Be Thankful in All Circumstances	Dissatisfaction With Own Life Compared to Lives of Screen Characters

the Scripture search on the Worksheet 1. You may have teens work individually or in groups. Sample answers are shown above.

Discuss the four priorities Paul gives for our time in Ephesians 5:15-20. Use the comments outlined in the *resource material*. Discuss the possible negative effects of excessive viewing. After this discussion share the following thoughts.

"Paul clearly defines what he means when he said to *'redeem the time.'* Instead of concentrating on the negative effects of TV and movies, let us look for ways to spend our time fulfilling Paul's commands."

THE LOST LETTER

Ask a teen to read aloud Ephesians 5:15-20. Lead the group in discussion of the phrase *"redeeming the time."* Help them to discover the four activities which Paul indicated as redeeming the time. Write these activities on the chalkboard or overhead transparency.

Then explain to teens that they have been made part of an archeological team that has been making some remarkable discoveries in the Middle East. Remnants of a great TV network of the Roman Empire (during the time of Paul) have been found and analyzed. Evidence indicates that the TV fare appealed to the masses, being saturated with themes of sex, violence, and the man-centered philosophy of the day (sound familiar?). This archeological team has discovered Paul's first draft copy of Ephesians 5:15-20. It seems that a member of the church, Videos Viewit, had been encouraging the members to spend all of their time watching the tube. In this version of Ephesians 5, Paul not only encouraged the Ephesians to redeem the time, but he also gave reasons why constant TV viewing kept them from fulfilling these commands.

Allow teens (either individually or in groups) ten to fifteen minutes to write a mythical letter to the videoholics of Ephesus. Encourage teens to share their letters with the entire group.

Call attention to the negative effects of excessive viewing as expressed in the letters. Include other effects if you feel that some important aspects have been missed. Then share the following thoughts.

"Although Paul did not face the exact problem that we have just discussed, I believe that you are correct in your application of his words to television viewing. Excessive viewing can keep us from understanding God's will, being filled with the Spirit, fellowshipping with God and our Christian brothers and sisters, and having an attitude of thanksgiving in the ways which you described. Now let us turn away from the negative effects toward some positive ways we can spend our time fulfilling the commands of Scripture."

RESPOND

Use one or more of the following activities to continue this session.

1. **"You Love the World & You're Avoiding Me!"**
Before Keith Green went to his new home in heaven, the Lord inspired him to write some of the most inspiring and challenging songs. Many of these songs are geared to motivate Christians to become active participants in their faith rather than just religious spectators. One of these songs called "You Love the World and You're Avoiding Me!" from the album, *So You Wanna Go Back to Egypt?,* talks about the time we spend with God developing our personal relationships with Him. The song is sung as if from Jesus' perspective. He is concerned because of the worldly things that we spend our time with—the light of our TVs, books, magazines, etc.—are leaving us no quality time to spend with Him. It is a very powerful song!!! Play the song at this time. Lead the group in some discussion about the validity of the message of this song.

Then, lead the group in a brain-storming discussion. Ask teens to list activities that would help them to understand God's will, be filled with the Spirit, have fellowship, and be thankful as Paul directed. A few possibilities include the following: having a daily devotional period, keeping a prayer journal, reading the Bible, commentaries, and Christian books and magazines, listening to Christian music, fellowshipping at Christian socials, and serving other people through projects. Use this list for one of the following activities.

2. **Movie Poster**
Since the early days of the motion picture show, movies have been successfully promoted by the use of poster advertising. Even today posters still hang outside and inside movie theatres and are often used as newspaper ads. For this activity, you will need several of these ads from the weekend newspaper.

Direct each teen to choose one item from the list made in the brain-storming discussion. Distribute poster paper and marking pens. Ask each teen to design a movie-type ad promoting his chosen activity. Encourage teens to use the same style as the movie ads. Attempting to make the activity appear as desirable as the movies seem to be. Ask group members to share their completed projects. Mount these projects on the walls of the classroom for the remainder of this unit.

3. **Prime Time Guide**
It would probably be surprising if it were known how many families are ruled by TV listings. Television has a way of monopolizing schedules and time. The purpose of this exercise is to enable teens to create their own scheduling, rather than allowing network programmers to do so.

Distribute Worksheet 2 at this time. Instruct teens to choose a few activities from the brain-storming list. The activities chosen should be activities which teens could do during the next week. Ask teens to schedule those activities for the evening hours. They should then list the other activities for which teens are normally responsible (for example: meal time, job, homework, household chores, and sleep). If there are any remaining time spots, allow teens to schedule some TV viewing.

CLOSING

Close the session by seriously discussing the posters or their prime time guides. Spend a moment in silent prayer, asking for God's help in scheduling activities which reflect His priorities. Ask a teen to close with an audible prayer.

SESSION 2

TV, MOViES, aND... YOUR RELaTiONSHiPS

OBJECTiVES

As a result of this session, teens should be able to do one or more of the following:

1. List the responsibilities of both parties in the following relationships:
   a. male/female
   b. parent/child
   c. employer/employee
2. Contrast the TV view of these relationships with the Biblical view, citing specific examples.
3. Pinpoint areas in their lives in which they are emulating a TV/movie life-style rather than a God-ordained life-style.

aDVaNCE PREPaRaTiON

1. Make copies of Worksheets 3 and 4 from the masters at the end of this unit.
2. Mount 2 six-foot lengths of newsprint on the wall and provide several markers if you choose the *Graffiti* activity.
3. Prepare 3 x 5 index cards for this session by following the instructions in the *Pet Peeve* activity.
4. Be sure to have plenty of Bibles, paper, and pencils available for use.
5. Make copies of the role play summaries in the *Respond* section for those who will participate.

MEETiNG SCHEDULE

Ready	10 minutes
Research	15 minutes
Respond	25 minutes
Closing	10 minutes

RESOURCE MaTERiaL

"Seeing is believing." Surely this maxim was coined far before the advent of movies and TV. However, this saying has a haunting new relevance since the birth of the television.

The moving pictures of the screen have an element which no other form of media possesses. We may sympathize or even empathize with a well-developed character in a novel. We may even comment that we know someone like him. But he is a character—a product of two imaginations (the reader's and the writer's), paper, and ink. The creations of a gifted artist may nearly breathe with life-like detail. But if you were to talk to the artist, he would probably talk about how *similar* his work is to the real thing. He is quite aware that he is only creating a facsimile of reality through his art work.

Enter the shimmering screen. Villains in soap operas receive very real hate mail. A star of a camera commercial sometimes wears a tee shirt denying that her co-star is her husband. A humorous story is told to visitors at a certain studio: A lady visitor was overcome with joy when she saw an actor who played a wheel-chair-bound detective walking on the back lot between takes. The screen has the power to convince some viewers that fantasy is reality.

"But," you object, "those are extreme cases! Most people are not affected that way!" Of course, these cases are rather extreme, but they are extreme in degree only. To a degree we are all vulnerable. We may have never been inside a courtroom, a police station, or the office of a corporate chief. But we can describe these places—we have a mental image of what they are like. Or, do we?

Sorry, but what we have is an image of an image. What we can describe is a Hollywood fantasy of a courtroom, police station, or exec-utive office—a fantasy which may or may not have any real correlation to the real item. And yet our intelligent minds have been mesmer-ized and charmed by the screen's spell.

This not only holds true concerning sights we have never seen but also concerning feelings we have never felt and relationships of which we have never been apart. Here in lies a deadly danger to all of us as Christians, but especially to Christian teenagers.

Many years before they begin an earnest search for a marriage partner, adolescents have already seen fantasy images of what both the search and the relationship should be. While most teens have only one home life, they have been bombarded with scores of other examples of family settings. Before joining the ranks of the employed, teens have seen images of fac-tory workers, business men, and agrarians. In the same way that we "know" an urban precinct station, so teenagers "know" what constitutes the ideal relationships. But does this "knowl-edge" really help teens to relate?

The apostle Paul addressed the church con-cerning these relationships. His picture is not one broadcast from a Hollywood fantasyland, but rather from the mind of the One who de-signed these relationships.

Unlike the popular images, the Biblical view of relationships is one of mutual submission rather than personal gratification. Paul's in-structions to the Ephesians were to *"be subject to one another out of reverence for Christ"* (Ephe-sians 5:21, *NIV*). This admonition establishes the divine standard flying above all human rela-tionships. It is this standard that every Christian should honor, rather than the seductive banner of the shimmering screen. But let us look at both sets of standards.

MaLe/FeMaLe ReLaTiONSHiPS

It seems that we have become numb to what TV and movies have done to the first human relationship, God's own creation. This numb-ness is seen even among committed Christians. In one particular family, the wife (who professes to be a committed disciple) avidly watched a

FAMILY RELATIONSHIPS

Parent/child relationships, as God intends, are also marked by two-way submission. This mutual submission stands in direct contrast to the family relationships which Hollywood designs.

The *cute kid* is the screen's child stereotype. Between the ages of eight and twelve (but "going on thirty"), this little stinker does what he or she wants when he or she wants. When Mom *or* Dad object (notice there is usually only one parent), the junior Don Rickles unloads with a blazing wit, reducing the parent to a heap of imbecilic ashes.

The parent depicted on the screen, other than being an idiot, is shamelessly self-absorbed. Whether it be to the job, the love-interest, or friends, the child's well-being is secondary.

In sharp contrast stands the Scriptural model. Children are to be obedient to parents. The result of this obedience is the security so obviously lacking in the life of the *cute kid* (Ephesians 6:1-3). Children are not to be treated as intrusions into parents' lives! Parents are to treat the discipline and instruction of their children as the very purpose of their existence (Ephesians 6:4; Colossians 3:21).

EMPLOYER/EMPLOYEE RELATIONSHIPS

Work depicted on the screen is either very glamorous or non-existent. Leisure time is the goal of living.

But the apostle Paul disagrees. Inspired by the Holy Spirit, Paul says, *"Serve wholeheartedly, as if you were serving the Lord, not men"* (Ephesians 6:7, *NIV*). Labor is not something to be avoided. Instead, work is to be entered into with a spirit of worship and service. The boss is not to be treated as a money-hungry buffon, but is to be respected (Ephesians 6:5). Neither is a boss to be "buttered-up" for the worker's personal gain (v. 6). Making the dramatic contrast with Hollywood style employees complete, the

popular television program. This show featured the trysts of a collection of people aboard a cruise ship. The relationships depicted were usually sexual in nature and nearly always without the benefit of marriage (at least to the current partner). The husband mentioned to his TV-viewing wife, "Honey, those folks are sinning." Her reflex action was one of defensiveness. But then she was filled with shock that she could have been so deceived. Adulterous relationships, served up by freshly scrubbed, people-next-door faces, are made to look as natural and wholesome as granola breakfast cereal!

The Biblical pattern for male/female relationships is not one based upon the shaky ground of personal pleasure. Paul obtains his imagery from the mutually submissive relationship of Christ and the church. As the church yields her will to the will of the Savior, so should the wife yield her search for personal gratification to her husband's will (Ephesians 5:22-24). Likewise as Christ yielded His personal desires for the good of the church, the man must be willing to sacrifice even his own life for his wife (Ephesians 5:25, 28). Unlike the popular portrait painted by the media, the love relationship must be characterized by mutual giving rather than by manipulation, conquest, and demand (Ephesians 5:33).

Christian worker is to exhibit a servant attitude, even if the employer is unreasonable and cruel (1 Peter 2:18).

But again the Biblical pattern is mutual submission. Respect for his employees is the mark of a Christian in charge. The popular image of some jobs with status and other jobs which are lowly is utterly rejected by an impartial God (Ephesians 6:9).

Teenagers must be taught to view critically the entertainment media. Rather than modeling the fantasies of Hollywood, teens must be led to choose the Scripture as God's norm for personal relationships.

Session Plan

Ready

Use one of the following activities to begin this session.

1. Graffiti

Tape two lengths of newsprint or white shelf paper (six feet each) to one wall of the room. Place three or four watercolor markers nearby. (Note: permanent markers will "bleed" through the paper, leaving marks on the wall.)

On top of one sheet, print the following words:

I LIKE IT WHEN PEOPLE ...

On top of the other sheet print these words:

I DON'T LIKE IT WHEN PEOPLE ...

As teens enter the room, direct them to that wall. Encourage teens to write down their first thoughts upon considering the phrases.

After the last graffito has been written, help teens to categorize the type of behavior they dislike or like in other people. Encourage such responses as the following: selfish, self-centered, ungrateful, submissive, understanding, selfless, appreciative, and other words that deal with being either self-centered or other-centered.

2. Pet Peeves

As teens enter the room, hand each one a 3 x 5 index card. Instruct them to write their "pet peeve" on that card and hand it back to you.

After all cards have been collected, share a few of them with the group. Try to emphasize those behaviors which illustrate selfishness rather than a concern for the feelings and rights of other people. Ask teens to pinpoint the nature of the attitude of people who commit such

offenses. Help them realize that they prefer people who are other-centered over those who are self-centered.

After using one of these activities, share the following thoughts.

"This discussion will look at the media's treatment of personal relationships. We have just mentioned some of the ways we like and do not like people to treat us. Let us see if the relationships between people on the media screen are the kinds which the Bible prescribes for us as Christians."

RESEARCH

Use one of the following activities to continue this session.

1. What Makes Good Relationships?

Divide teens into three groups. Ask each group to select a leader and scribe. Distribute Worksheet 3. Each leader will ask members of the group to read the Scriptures on the worksheet and work together on an essay. The assigned topics are as follows:

Group 1—"What makes a good male/female relationship?"
Group 2—"What makes good family relationships?"
Group 3—"What makes good work relationships?"

After about fifteen minutes, have the groups read their essays aloud. Open discussion on each topic. Enlarge the discussion by using information contained in the resource material. Ask for examples of each relationship from popular movies or television programs. Discuss how these relationships may differ from Biblical examples. Note that the Biblical command to *"submit to one another out of reverence for Christ"* (Ephesians 5:21, *NIV*) is the key to making all three of these relationships work properly and effectively.

2. Advise to the Stars

Divide the teens into three groups. Select the

story lines of three popular TV programs or movies as examples of faulty male/female, family, and work relationships. An ideal situation would exist if you knew someone who had a small library of movies or TV programs. If these were videotaped, you could show one minute "clips" of each relationship listed.

Assign each group a problem and ask the groups to show how an application of Biblical principles would alleviate the problems. Proceed in the same way as described in the previous activity.

RESPOND

When introducing either of the following activities, share the following thoughts.

"We can see that the way life's relationships are portrayed on the screen often runs counter to the way God would have us to live. We need to determine whether our relationships are patterned after the screen or are focused on the Word of God."

CHECKLIST

Distribute Worksheet 4. Instruct teens to respond thoughtfully to the questions listed. Give them approximately five minutes to complete this exercise. Discussion should be discouraged during this time because teens should be doing some serious introspection. Make certain they know that the results will not be shared.

After everyone has marked the checklist, allow some time for discussion. Ask the group, "To what extent is your negative behavior, in your relationships with other people, affected by what you see in movies or on television?"

Teens should determine whether the portrayal of commitment-free relationships with members of the opposite sex causes teens to be less considerate of their boyfriend or girlfriend. Many children on television situation comedies are known for snappy comebacks to parents. Have teens ever found themselves sounding like these television characters when speaking to their own parents? Likewise, since many programs depict parents as incompetent, have teenagers ever doubted their parents' judg-

ments? Have teenagers ever subconsciously believed that this TV image was an accurate portrayal of their own family? Have media images of successful and affluent young people made teenagers feel somewhat resentful that they had to perform some mundane chores or tedious work?

ROLE PLAYS

Do as many role plays as time allows. Ask for volunteers for each skit. Ask actors to play the scene two times—the first time as it might be depicted on a TV situation comedy, and the second time according to the Scriptural directives of Ephesians 5:21-6:9. If you have a number of willing volunteers, you may choose to use different characters in the second scene. Allow for discussion after the role play situation has been presented both ways. Encourage teens to share instances where teens acted more like a television or movie character than the example of Jesus Christ.

Ask teens to make up their own role plays. Anyone who has viewed much television has seen lots of possible scenes!

NOW COMES THE REAL FUN-N-GAMES

Role Play 1

The scene takes place in Mr. and Mrs. Funingames' living room. The scene opens as Mrs. Funingames returns from a shopping trip. Against her husband's wishes, Mrs. Funingames has purchased boxes upon boxes of new clothes for herself. Mr. Funingames is sitting in the living room with his back to the door when she enters the room.

Role Play 2

The scene takes place in Del's Diner. Waitress Deara brings a cup of hot coffee to a customer. Before she can set the cup on the table, the bottom of the paper cup gives way, and the hot coffee spills on the table and the customer. Del runs out of the kitchen to come to the aid of the customer. (You may not want to cast anyone as the customer. If you do, have him remain silent. The crucial conversation is the one between Del and Deara.)

Role Play 3

It is Sunday afternoon and Starchie Clunker is watching a football game. He is in the living room with his son-in-law Mick (whom Starchie calls, in his less charitable moments, "Bonehead"). Mick remarks that violent games such as football are the reason why the United States is militarily involved in conflict in Central America. Since politics is a topic upon which the two men strongly disagree, an argument ensues. Starchie's daughter enters and attempts to break up the argument.

CLOSING

Instruct teens to be mindful of the relationships between men and women, parent and child, and employer and employee in any television program that teens may watch during the next week. Encourage teens to pray *on the spot* if they see any behavior in the screen relationships that teens have also been modeling.

Form a prayer circle and ask each teen to say a one sentence prayer. Prayer may be directed toward asking God's guidance concerning viewing choices. Teens might also ask God to give them His vision.

Session 3

TV, Movies, and... Your Mind

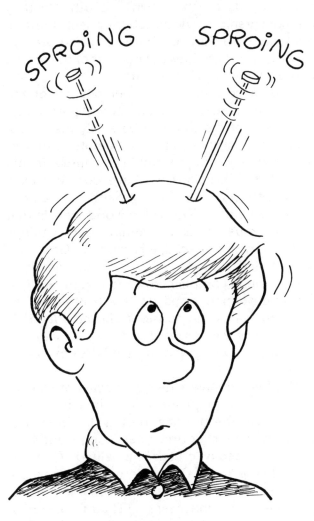

SPROING   SPROING

Objectives

As a result of this session, teens should be able to do one or more of the following:

1. Recognize that TV/movies often present a world view at odds with a Biblical viewpoint.
2. Describe and give examples of the popular TV/movie view of God, man, and sin.
3. Contrast the above view with the Biblical view on the same subjects.
4. Conclude that TV/movies affect some important perceptions of themselves and other people.

Advance Preparation

1. Make copies of Worksheets 5 and 6, and the script from the masters at the end of this unit.
2. Bring enough cardboard tubes (paper towel or bathroom tissue tubes) for each teen if you use the *Tunnel Vision* activity.
3. Bring one board game for every 4-6 teens in the group. The games should be unfamiliar to them. You will also need to remove one small but crucial, instruction or game piece. These will be used in the *Lame Games* activity.
4. Recruit someone to portray Mr. T.V. Tube in the skit. They will need a copy of the script and enough time to devise a costume.
5. If you use the *Revealing Reports* activity in the *Research* section, you will need to make assignments to 3 teens early in the week. See the *Revealing Reports* activity for further details.
6. Contact an adult sponsor from the junior age youth group to complete the survey information for use with the *Respond* activity.

Meeting Schedule

Ready	15 minutes
Research	15 minutes
Respond	20 minutes
Closing	10 minutes

Resource Material

"Who has known the mind of the Lord?" wrote the apostle Paul, *"or who has been his counselor?"* (Romans 11:34, *NIV*). Paul warns that Christians should not conform their minds to

WHAT'S ON THE FUNNEL, TONIGHT?

HOLLYWOOD

current philosophies and values. The way to do this is to be *"transformed by the renewing of your mind"* (Romans 12:2), in order to be within God's will.

Television and movies have an influence on our minds that is shared by no other form of communication. The screen is a funnel, with the large end pointed toward Hollywood, and the small end positioned in our living rooms. The communication process is only one-way. We absorb, but we do not express.

The problem arises when we realize that the view of the world funneled into our homes differs considerably from the mind of the Lord. Christian philosophers say that people often *catch* their world view in the way people *catch* a cold—exposure. If that idea is true, then TV and movies have started an epidemic.

Although the areas at which the video world view diverges from the Christian world view are numerous, a few areas are more significant than the differing views of God, man, and sin.

THE VIDEO VIEW OF GOD

TV and movies rarely mention God or a religious faith. But omission is not to be construed as neutrality. Remember the words of Jesus:

"He that is not with me is against me" (Matthew 12:30). The silence of the screen speaks volumes.

Televisionland abounds with strong characters and hero types. They save lives, rescue lovely women, and apprehend dangerous criminals. Those heroes, however, perform their heroic deeds on their own strength. Do they attend worship services? Do they seek spiritual guidance? Do they ask for strength in prayer? Clearly, such activities are not part of the screen heroes' lives or priority systems.

What a contrast to the perspective of the Bible! God is seen to be an integral part of life, not a part of life that can be easily discarded. God is not removed in some remote corner or life (as He is often ignored in the unreal media world.) As Christians we have our very existence with Him (Acts 17:28). Neither is He powerless to help us. The video world view is that the strong person can accomplish great things and perform heroic deeds without God. Yet, persons with the mind of Christ know that *nothing* can be accomplished without Him. An Old Testament verse sums up this truth—*"Unless the Lord builds the house, its builders labor in vain. Unless the Lord watches over the city, the watchmen stand guard in vain"* (Psalm 127:1, NIV).

The few positive video portrayals of sincere faith appear in programs with a nostalgic setting. On the prairies, during the Great Depression, whenever times were rough, and individuals needed a "crutch"—a belief in God was there. In the age of the modern, self-made man, however, such practices are considered old-fashioned and unnecessary. Though unstated, the message is obvious.

The Biblical reality stands 180 degrees opposed to the video fantasy. We serve an unchanging Lord. His nature is the same yesterday, and today, and forever (Hebrews 13:8). His word is eternal (1 Peter 1:25). Our need for Him has equal longevity.

Probably the most disturbing feature of TV's portrait of God is the open hostility to organized religion which surfaces occasionally. The preacher who is a swindler . . . the Bible-toting Army major who also carries on an adulterous relationship with an equally "pious" nurse . . . the mugger who leaves a Bible next to his victims. The message from Hollywood is clear: believers are not only weak and old-fashioned, but they are also ulteriorly motivated, hypocritical, or just plain deranged. According to the video world view, being around Christians could be dangerous!

The splash of the Living Water awakens us from this small-screen nightmare and refreshes us with truth. It is true that some people have shipwrecked their faith (1 Timothy 1:19). Yet, Christians remain the hope of the world, not its scourge. We serve a God Who helps us to overcome, not a God who seeks to hurt and destroy us (Romans 8:31-39).

THE VIDEO VIEW OF MAN

In the world of television, only certain people are deemed important enough for prime time programs. An overview of the tube's population sees it disproportionately *stacked* with rich, young city dwellers. If a person does not fall into this category, he has little appeal to the viewing audience, and hence, is of little value.

But the mind of the Lord is not the mid of the screen. All men are created in God's image (Genesis 1:26). Salvation is desired by God for all people (2 Peter 3:9). The wealthy are not more worthy than the poor (James 2:1-7). God shows no partiality (Acts 10:34-35).

THE VIDEO VIEW OF SIN

Sin!!! Our tolerant society does not like that word! It comes as no surprise that this word is also unwelcome on the glowing box and the silver screen. Acceptance is the prevailing theme. The TV tube would have us to believe that there is no right or wrong, only differences in preferences and life-styles.

The unreal world of TV and movies pours into most homes on a daily basis. Counterfeit portrayals of God, man, and sin have been blindly accepted as true by many TV viewers. How do we protect ourselves and other people from these false impressions?

A story is told about a bank manager's system of discovering phony bills. Instead of teaching bank tellers about the possible imperfections of counterfeit bills, he had tellers concentrate on the features of genuine bills. *Our task is clear*—we must concentrate on the reality that the Father has revealed. Then we will be more apt to discern falsehood, be it presented in dancing phosphor dots or in any other fashion!

SESSION PLAN

READY

Use one of the following activities to begin this session.

1. Tunnel Vision

Hand a cardboard tube to each teen. Instruct them to close one eye and hold the tube to the other eye with their left hand. Upon your signal, teens are to get up from their seats and shake hands with ten people *as fast as they can.*

Tunnel Vision can be a wild activity. Keep teens (especially junior highers) somewhat calm to avoid getting carried away. Yet, this activity must be a bit chaotic to make a point.

After this activity is finished, calm everyone down again and straighten any items which were *rearranged* during the activity. When everyone has caught their breath, share the following thoughts.

a Lame Game

"That was not easy to do. It seems that we need to see the entire picture before doing even the simplest tasks. The cardboard tubes limited our vision. To function as true disciples, we need to be able to view the entire picture of life. The Bible calls this viewpoint and perspective as having *the mind of Christ.* In this session, we will discuss some ways in which TV and movies limit our vision and keep us from seeing all of life with the mind of God."

2. Lame Games

Cluster teens into groups of 5-6. Hand a board game to each group, and instruct them to begin playing that game. The game should be one with which teens are not familiar. They should have to read the instructions to learn how to play. Before the session begins, you will need to prepare the games by removing a small, but crucial, item (i.e., a paragraph of instructions or a game piece). Meander among the groups to determine how each group is progressing. If a teen asks a question about the missing part, apologize, but tell them to figure out how to manage without the part.

After frustration builds, put the games away, and reassemble them into one large group. Then, share the following thoughts.

"We all realize how frustrating it is to try to play a game when a piece is missing. Sure, we can try to make do, but it just is not the same as playing with a complete game. Life is also very frustrating if some of the pieces are gone. As Christians, we have all of the pieces of life available to us if we view life with what the Bible calls the *mind of Christ.* In this session, we will look at the world, as presented by TV and movies, to identify some pieces that are missing."

RESEARCH

Use one of the following activities to continue the session.

1. Interview with Mr. T.V. Tube

Before the session, secure a volunteer (either a teen or an adult) to be *Mr. T.V. Tube.* A mask

designed to look like a TV set can be fashioned from a small cardboard box. Make certain the volunteer is familiar with the script (found in the supplemental pages at the end of this unit). He need not memorize it word-for-word, as long as he knows the gist of the responses. The interview will be more effective if not read.

Introduce Mr. Tube to the class, and then explain that he agreed to the interview so that the group would know his own views on important matters. The interview is to be conducted in fun, but at the same time, serious information will be presented. You, as the interviewer, can help set that tone.

After the interview, thank Mr. Tube and send him on his way. Then, distribute Worksheet 5. Either individually or in groups, teens should find the Scripture references and fill in the chart. Discuss the differences between the mind of the screen and the mind of God (in reference to the subjects covered). Then, share the following thoughts.

"It seems obvious that the video viewpoint and the Biblical viewpoint are quite different on the subjects of God, man, and sin. In Romans 12:2, Paul warns us not to be conformed to the world, but to have our minds renewed to understand God's will. Let us see to what degree that minds are conformed to the world rather than being transformed by God. Then, let us deter-mine what we can do about transforming our minds."

2. Revealing Reports

A few days before this session, you will need to ask three teens to prepare oral reports. These young people need to be fairly familiar with televised fare. They are to research their assignment by surveying the TV listings and/or reporting on the programs watched during the week. Here are the assignments.

Assignment 1

By surveying the TV listings and your knowledge of prime time series, be ready to answer the following questions as an oral report.

1. How many TV shows have a main character who has a strong religious faith?
2. How many series (that you know of) have *no* characters who show any religious faith?
3. Of those shows with religious characters, how many series are set in modern times, and how many series take place in the past?
4. Of those shows with religious characters, how many of those characters are portrayed positively, and how many are portrayed negatively?
5. Describe the negative characteristics given to the religious character.

6. From the above evidence, what seems to be television's view of religion?

Assignment 2

By surveying the TV listings and your own knowledge of prime time TV series, be ready to answer the following questions as an oral report.

1. Compare the number of series whose lead characters come from urban areas.
2. Compare the number of series whose lead characters are richer than the average person to the number of series whose lead characters are poorer than the average person.
3. Compare the number of series whose lead characters are younger than your parents to the number of series whose lead characters are older than your parents.
4. Does TV seem to show partiality between rich and poor? Small towns and big cities? Old and young? Explain your answers.

Assignment 3

Be ready to give the following oral report. Describe two or three television plots that you have watched in which behavior that the Bible describes as sin was accepted or even justified. What is TV's view of sin? Is there such a thing as sin? Is it to be taken seriously?

Call on these three young people to present their oral reports. After their reports are given, ask all teens if these reports seem accurate. Encourage free discussion and supplement with your own comments.

RESPOND

TV, MOVIES, AND THE YOUNGER GENERATION

Before this session, you will need to contact the adult sponsor of the junior (grades 4-6) youth group. Ask the sponsor if he (or she) would distribute cards to the junior youth group. These cards should have the following directions written on them:

"List your five most admired celebrities."

Ask the adult sponsor if the completed cards could be delivered to you prior to this session.

Distribute Worksheet 6 to the group. Explain that an important task of adulthood is even now becoming a teenage responsibility. This important task involves teaching and influencing (through role modeling) younger people to develop the mind of Christ. Describe the nature of the informal survey involving the junior youth group. Tell the teens that you would like their help in analyzing the survey results. Read the celebrities' names listed while the teens write those names on the proper worksheet columns. They should categorize the names as political leaders, religious leaders, TV/movie characters or music stars, or others.

Discuss the results of this survey with teens. Do TV/movie stars play a prominent role in the list? Greater than the religious figures? Greater than the political people? Is this influence more likely to cause young people to "conform to the world" or to "be transformed by the renewing of their minds?" What kind of examples do they set for younger children? Would their lists be similar to the junior youth groups' lists? Do Christians need to become more aware of how the media influences decisions about who and what are important?

CLOSING

Close the session by reading Romans 11:33-12:2. You may read it, a teen may read it, or if you have enough copies of the same translation, the group may read this passage chorally as follows. Then close with a time of prayer.

All:	11:33
Leader:	11:34
Teens:	11:35
All:	11:36
Leader:	12:1
All:	12:2

Session 4

TV, Movies, and... Your Choices

Objectives

As a result of this session, teens should be able to do one or more of the following:

1. Recognize that 1 Corinthians 10:23-33 is a measuring rod for determining which activities are acceptable.
2. Evaluate reasons for watching or not watching TV and movies.
3. Decide whether or not watching their favorite TV shows/movies glorifies God.
4. List possible ways of controlling their viewing habits.

Advance Preparation

1. Make copies of Worksheets 7 and 8 from the masters at the end of this unit.
2. Prepare 3 x 5 index cards according to the instructions in the *Scripture Assembly* activity if you decide to use it.
3. Bring extra paper, markers or colored pencils for the *Cartoon Strip* activity if you decide to use it.
4. Make sure there are plenty of Bibles, paper, and pencils available for use.

Meeting Schedule	
Ready	10 minutes
Research	20 minutes
Respond	20 minutes
Closing	10 minutes

Resource Material

When it comes to the entertainment media, probably the most thought provoking question we, as Christians, need to deal with is this—*"To what extent can we as God's people be involved with the prevailing culture of our secular society?"*

The question is a complex one and is dealt with in detail by several Christian authors. This session's purpose is to find some type of *acid test,* a Biblical principle, which Christians can use to evaluate their personal viewing habits.

Although it did not deal with entertainment, a similar problem arose during Paul's time. This problem dealt with the extent to which Christians could be involved with the pagan culture surrounding them. The question concerned the propriety of eating meat and came about due to cultural practices. As was the practice of Judaism, the practitioners of paganism also sacrificed animals to their gods. In Corinth, the meat from the sacrificed animals was often sold in the market place. What a dilemma for Christians in that society! How could a person tell whether or not the meat he purchased had been dedicated to a pagan god? Would eating meat that had been used for pagan sacrifices turn followers of Christ into idol worshipers? Should a buyer first ask the seller about the history of a steak before purchasing it? What if the merchant lies just to make the sale? Or should Christians just have stopped eating meat altogether? The issue was not as simple as it might seem at first.

Christians at Corinth held differing opinions on this controversy. Some believers felt that total abstinence from meat was in order. Other Christians then countered with, "I am a Christian, so no legalistic rules bind me. I can do as I please."

Paul was inspired by God to respond to his controversy in a manner that mediated these two man-made opinions in 1 Corinthians 10:23, 31 (NIV): "Everything is permissible"—but not everything is beneficial. "Everything is permissible"—but not everything is constructive ... So whether you eat or drink or whatever you do, do it all for the glory of God.

On the one hand, the apostle Paul did agree with the meat-eaters. He said that eating whatever was sold in the marketplace was acceptable, as long as the partaker was thankful to God for his food (1 Corinthians 10:30). But on the other hand, Paul rejected the self-indulgence of believers who argued that because of the salvation they had received, they could then do as they pleased. Paul was emphatic in his exhortation: believers are responsible to each other. Freedom was not to be flaunted at someone else's expense (1 Corinthians 10:24).

The question of how Christians should relate to current entertainment options has more facets than could be reasonably covered in this session. But Paul's principles continue to prove useful. Do our choices of entertainment help us or other people in some way? Do we glorify God in our video viewing?

The following are some challenges and also practical applications, based simply on the "Corinthian Acid Test."

INVENTORY

The first three sessions revealed how excessive and unwise viewing could be detrimental. Television and movies can waste our time, befuddle our relationships, and subvert our world views. Of course, some video programs are more obvious offenders than others.

A modern application of Paul's words to the Corinthians is for contemporary Christians to inventory their personal viewing habits. Ask yourself these questions: How many hours per week is the box in the living room turned on? Do I ever find myself turning on the tube just to have something to do? Do I watch whatever program is on, or am I more selective? Am I being harmed by the ideas of anything that I watch? Am I comfortable that God knows my thoughts as I view television programs?

In business practices, an inventory often causes a manager to alter his purchasing patterns and convinces him to sell overstocked items. Likewise, our viewing inventory may urge us to behave in a similar fashion.

VIDEO FAST

Many people are shocked when they discover that viewing has become a powerful addiction for them. After tallying the number of hours spend watching TV or movies, we may choose to do something rather drastic to free us from dependence on TV.

Three types of video fasts are possible—total, temporary, and selective. A total fast is rare but not without merit. Some people decide that they do not want the distraction of television in their homes, and so they get rid of their box. The temptation to be a video glutton is gone. But the drawback to this approach is that it eliminated the possibility of any worthwhile viewing at home.

A temporary fast is another alternative. Many

viewers wonder, "Will I miss TV?" To answer that question, a viewer pledges to go *cold turkey* for a pre-arranged period of time. After that period passes, viewers may be more apt to watch from volition rather than habit.

A selective fast is similar to Lenten observances. Instead of abstaining from all television on a permanent or temporary basis, a person may sacrifice a favorite program or viewing time. A selective fast can provide more time for expressly spiritual pursuits and activities. The adjustment time is perhaps easiest with a selective fast because it allows for a more gradual transition.

QUOTA

A quota approach would entail designating no more than a proportion of one's weekly time to viewing TV. The best way to handle this approach is with a weekly schedule. At the beginning of each week, a schedule of allowable viewing times would be designed. Another alternative is to view a maximum number of hours per week, and when those hours are reached, the set is then turned off for the rest of the week.

TV THINKBACK

Up to this point, we have only been considering ways to control negative viewing. However, Paul also encouraged the interaction with a pagan medium for a means of glorifying God. A potentially positive approach to video entertainment is to view a program through God's eyes. When viewing a TV show, focus in on the major theme. Just what does the Bible say about the treatment of that theme? Does the Biblical view differ from how the TV scriptwriter depicts the issue? After the program is over, try to find relevant Scripture passages. A Bible concordance and/or a topical Bible may be useful for this research project.

THINKER

THINKEE

ACTION

After attempting to view TV and movies through God's eyes, we may desire to see more programs which present positive values. One method of effecting positive change is to write thought-provoking letters to TV stations and movie studios. The letters should detail your objections to specific movies or TV programs, with possible suggestions for improvement.

The question of intermingling Christian values with contemporary entertainment is a controversy destined to be debated for a long time. Applying Paul's words to these controversies, however, is an appropriate beginning to allowing the Lord to reign in all areas of our lives—even all those hours spent before the glowing TV tube and the shimmering movie screen.

SESSION PLAN

READY

Use one of the following activities to begin this session.

1. Search 'N Scramble

Distribute Worksheet 7 and direct teens' attention to the *Search 'N Scramble* activity. They are to search the box for letters under the same numerals. After they have grouped the letters in the box according to their numbers, each group of letters needs to be unscrambled. The decoded phrase will read, *"All things are lawful, but not all things are helpful."* After teens have solved the puzzle, share the following thoughts with the group.

"We have seen in the past weeks that TV and movie viewing is not simply a matter of right and wrong. Our viewing choice can be either helpful or detrimental to our lives in Jesus. In this session, we will talk about our choices in regard to the entertainment media. How can our use of TV and movies be helpful to other people, uplifting to ourselves, and glorifying to God?"

2. Scripture Assembly

Write the words of 1 Corinthians 10:31 on 3 x 5 index cards, with one word on each card. Make enough sets for each group of 5-6 people.

To begin the session, divide the teens into small groups, giving each group a jumbled set of cards. Give teens a few minutes to assemble the words into a meaningful sentence. (Hopefully, the sentence will be the words of Paul in 1 Corinthians 10:31!) When everyone is done, share the following thoughts.

"We have a responsibility to use our lives to the glory of the One Who made us. In the past few weeks, we have discussed many drawbacks of excessive TV and movie viewing. In this session, we will discuss our choices regarding viewing habits, and ways viewing choices can glorify God."

RESEARCH

Use one of the following activities to continue the session.

1. Debate

Choose a responsible teen to help you organize and moderate a debate on the proposition: *"A Christian should not watch TV or go to movies."* Allow the teenager to assume a leadership role as much as possible.

Divide the teens into two groups. For maximum learning in a debate, request that they *argue against what they have already come to believe.* That way, teens can become more aware of the arguments against their point of view. This awareness will help them to solidify or rethink their original viewpoint.

In this situation, make sure that the most avid viewers argue the *pro* side of the argument while those teens who view less TV argue the *con* side.

Refer each side to the Scripture references on the worksheet. Give teens adequate time for research. Explain that a spokesperson for each group will be given a total of six minutes—four minutes to present his group's side and then two minutes to refute the opponent's arguments.

After the debate, you should clarify the two positions. Help teenagers to resolve the conflict by referring to two Bible chapters—1 Corinthians 10 and Romans 14. Indicate that a compromise can be reached by considering the issues of freedom and responsibility.

2. Scripture Paraphrase

Distribute paper to teenagers. Ask them to locate 1 Corinthians 10:23-33. Select one person to read aloud this section. Take time to explain the conflict about eating meat offered to idols.

Ask teens to paraphrase verses 23-24 and verses 31-33, substituting references concerning meat with references to watching TV and movies.

RESPOND

Use one of the following activities to continue the session.

1. Evaluating My Favorites

Spend a few moments reviewing themes of the past three sessions—the effects of TV and movie viewing upon the use of our time, our relationships with each other, and our view of the world.

Distribute Worksheet 8. Ask teens to list their five favorite movies or television programs (in any combination) on the worksheet chart. Give teens time to evaluate their choices thoughtfully, according to the guidelines of this unit. Before beginning this activity, tell them that these evaluations will not be collected or shared with the group.

After everyone has finished listing and evaluating, encourage teens to take their worksheets home with them. Ask them to pray daily for guidance about their viewing habits and choices. Teens should also ask God to remove any stumbling blocks which might hinder them from making wise choices.

2. Cartoon Strips

Discuss the necessity of glorifying God in all of our actions, including our TV viewing habits.

Take a few minutes to explain the possible approaches to controlling TV viewing as described in the *resource material* for this session. List these approaches on the chalkboard. Encourage teens to think of other ways to control TV viewing.

Divide the group into partners. Give each pair four sheets of paper on which to create a four panel cartoon strip. The purpose of the cartoon is to show a person trying to use one of the suggested approaches listed on the chalkboard. The cartoon should depict both the approach used and the results. Ask the pairs to share their cartoons with the group.

CLOSING

As this session comes to a close, ask several teens to lead in a time of prayer. Encourage them to pray for God's guidance and direction as we make choices about our video viewing.

Time Schedule

You are awake about 100 hours ever week. Estimate below how many hours you spend doing each activity.

_____ School Attendance/Homework   _____ TV/Movies
_____ Hobbies/Sports   _____ Work (at Home or Job)
_____ Social Functions   _____ Other
_____ Bible Reading/Prayer/Church

                                Total _____

Scripture Search

Scripture	Activity Commanded	How Does Excessive TV or Movie Viewing Hinder?
Ephesians 5:17 Colossians 1:9 Ephesians 1:9		
Ephesians 5:18 Galatians 5:16 Ephesians 3:16		
Ephesians 5:19 Colossians 3:16 Hebrews 10:24, 25 1 Thessalonians 5:11		
Ephesians 5:20 Colossians 3:17 1 Thessalonians 5:18		

Permission to reproduce individual worksheets granted.

PRiMe TiMe GuiDe

Schedule Some "Time-Redeeming" Activities Into Next Week's Schedule.

	7:00-7:30 p.m.	7:30-8:00 p.m.	8:00-8:30 p.m.	8:30-9:00 p.m.	9:00-9:30 p.m.	9:30-10:00 p.m.	10:00-10:30 p.m.	10:30-11:00 p.m.
Monday								
Tuesday								
Wednesday								
Thursday								
Friday								
Saturday								
Sunday								

BUZZ GROUPS/ADVICE TO THE STARS

Consider the groupings of Scriptures below. Read and refer to them in describing God's standards for each category of relationships.

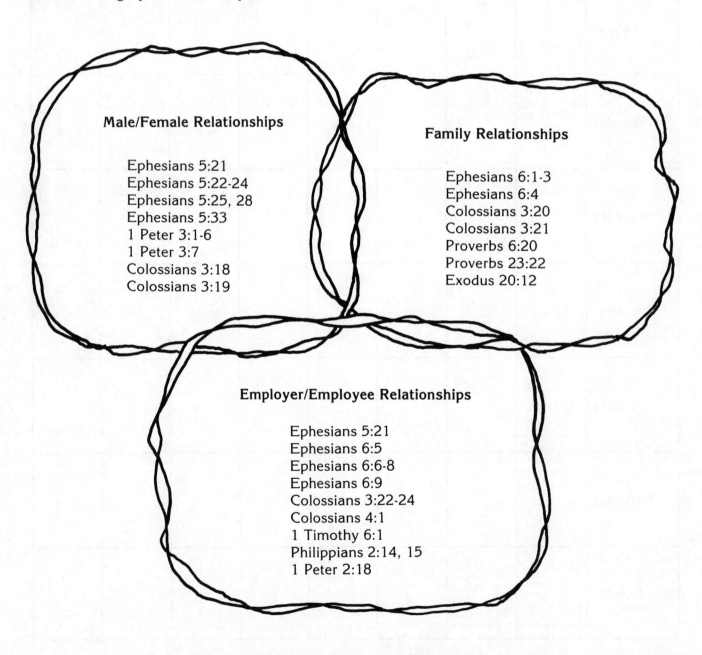

Male/Female Relationships

Ephesians 5:21
Ephesians 5:22-24
Ephesians 5:25, 28
Ephesians 5:33
1 Peter 3:1-6
1 Peter 3:7
Colossians 3:18
Colossians 3:19

Family Relationships

Ephesians 6:1-3
Ephesians 6:4
Colossians 3:20
Colossians 3:21
Proverbs 6:20
Proverbs 23:22
Exodus 20:12

Employer/Employee Relationships

Ephesians 5:21
Ephesians 6:5
Ephesians 6:6-8
Ephesians 6:9
Colossians 3:22-24
Colossians 4:1
1 Timothy 6:1
Philippians 2:14, 15
1 Peter 2:18

Permission to reproduce individual worksheets granted.

Check List

Honestly consider each of the following items. Mark those areas where you feel that you are model-ing a TV/movie life-style instead of a Christ-centered life-style. Take the list home and attempt to work on problem areas.

_____ 1. I often think of my girl friend/boyfriend in terms of how she/he can please me rather than how I can help her/him.

_____ 2. I sometimes envy the male/female relationships of promiscuous TV/movie characters.

_____ 3. I sometimes try to be like a promiscuous TV/movie character.

_____ 4. I like feeling that I am "in charge" in a male/female relationship.

_____ 5. I often resent my parents telling me what to do.

_____ 6. I often wonder if my parents know what they are doing.

_____ 7. I think of the time when I will have children so I can tell *them* what to do.

_____ 8. I resent doing hard manual work.

_____ 9. I often wonder if my boss (or teacher) knows what he/she is doing.

_____ 10. I think of the time when I will be in charge so I can boss people around.

INTERVIEW/REPORTS FOLLOW UP

Locate the listed references and contrast the Bible view with the current view of God, man, and sin.

TOPIC	THE MIND OF GOD	TV/MOVIE VIEW
God Acts 17:28 Hebrews 13:8 Romans 8:31-39		
Man Genesis 1:26 Acts 10:34, 35 James 2:1-7		
Sin Romans 3:23 Romans 6:23 Matthew 7:13, 14		

Permission to reproduce individual worksheets granted.

TV, Movies, & THE YOUNGER GENERATION

Your leader will read the names of people that members of a younger youth group in your church admire most; list the name under the correct heading.

TV/MOVIE STARS OR CHARACTERS	
OTHER ENTERTAINERS	POLITICAL FIGURES
RELIGIOUS FIGURES	OTHERS

search'n scramble

Decode a "mystery phrase," using the following steps:
1) Search out all the letters listed under the same numeral and write them in the appropriate place.
2) Then unscramble each word to produce the "mystery phrase."

1	6	4	8	3	10	7	10	8	3	9
L	O	W	S	R	E	L	P	T	A	E

10	9	5	4	8	2	10	4	4	7	8
H	R	U	F	N	S	L	L	L	A	G

6	9	2	5	2	8	4	10	1	7	2
N	A	G	B	T	H	A	L	A	L	I

10	6	2	5	1	10	4	8	3	11	2
U	T	N	T	L	U	F	U	E	.	H

_ _ _ _ _ _ _ _ _ _ _ _ _ _ _ _
  1   2   3   4

_ _ _ _ _ _ _ _ _ _ _ _
  5   6   7   8

_ _ _ _ _ _ _ _ _ _
    9   10   11

Debate

Study the Scriptures below to prepare a debate on the topic: *Resolved—A Christian should not watch television or go to movies.*

Pro:
Romans 12:1, 2
Ephesians 5:16
1 Thessalonians 5:22
Romans 16:19
Philippians 4:8
1 John 2:15
1 Corinthians 10:23

Con:
1 Corinthians 9:19-22
John 17:15
Galatians 5:1
1 Corinthians 10:23

Permission to reproduce individual worksheets granted.

evaluating my favorites

TV Program or Movie	Would people doubt my faith if they knew I watched this?	Does watching this affect how I view God, man, or sin?	Does watching this affect the way I treat others?	Could I be doing something more constructive?

TiME SCHEDULE

(Based on 100 Waking Hours/Week)
(Each Increment = Five Hours)

a. School/Homework   _____

b. Hobbies/Sports   _____

c. Social Functions   _____

d. Bible Reading/Prayer/   _____
    Church

e. TV/Movies   _____

f. Work (At Home or Job)   _____

g. Other   _____

Total   _____

INTERVIEW WITH MR. T.V. TUBE

Interviewer: Mr. T.V. Tube, as we have invited you here tonight to hear your opinions on some matters that concern us.

Mr. T.V. TUBE: Well, you're on the air! I'll be glad to answer any questions you have.

Interviewer: Thank you, T.V. We are interested in your opinion of God and religion.

Mr. TV: Well, my electronic eye sees the belief in God as a personal thing, so I really don't give it too much importance.

Interviewer: Not important?

Mr. TV: No, not really. The strong characters on my screen depend upon themselves rather than God.

Interviewer: Then you don't have any religious characters?

Mr. TV: Well, sometimes religious folks are on my channels, but they usually live during a period when times are tough. On the western prairie in the 1800-'s or on a Virginia mountain during the Great Depression, my characters leaned on a belief in God. But in modern days, such belief is rather old-fashioned.

Interviewer: Then religious characters are a thing of the past for you?

Mr. TV: For the most part. I do tune in to religious people now and then in a modern setting, but they usually give me trouble.

Interviewer: How so?

Mr. TV: I see cult members and narrow-minded hypocritical preachers trying to get rich. Modern-day religion seems a bit dangerous to me.

Interviewer: I see. So God is for weak, old-fashioned, and narrow-minded people.

Mr. TV: I just call 'em as my antennae sees 'em.

Interviewer: What are people like according to you?

Mr. TV: I like to show people that are important.

Interviewer: And who would that be?

Mr. TV: My favorites are rich, young people who live in big cities.

Interviewer: Tell us more.

Mr. TV: The Nielsens and I like people to be happy. So I show 'em folks who have it made ... lots of doctors, lawyers, and wealthy businessmen. My characters have plenty of time and money to show my viewers a good time.

Interviewer: Very interesting. Why do you like young people?

Mr. TV: Young people bring in new ideas. Teenagers change things. I've already told you what I think of old-fashioned ideas. Young! New! Exciting! That's what I like!

Interviewer: What's so special about big cities?

Mr. TV: Oh, you know how small town people are. Give me the action of a big city any day over a sleepy, old-fashioned small town.

Interviewer: So you are partial to certain groups of people. What do you think of sin?

Mr. TV: Shhhhhh! Don't say that word so loudly!

Interviewer: That's not a popular word with you?

Mr. TV: Not at all! That idea is older than my grandfather the radio!

Interviewer: So there is no right and wrong with you?

Mr. TV: The biggest wrong is when people take a religious stand on an issue. Live and let live! That kind of thinking is on my wavelength!

Interviewer: Mr. Tube, we thank you for your time. Your ideas are very revealing!

Habits: Making Them and Breaking Them

By Ward Patterson

Introduction

A man disappears and his family notifies the Missing Persons Bureau. The Bureau begins to make a profile of the man. What kind of things does he do, what kinds of things does he like? In short, the key to his whereabouts and identification is very likely to lie within his habits of conduct and his way of thinking.

All of us are creatures of habit. Our personal mannerisms, our preferences, our skills, our social graces, and our life-styles all partake of the nature of habit. Much of education is the imparting of useful habits of thought and conduct, whether it be the multiplication table or computer science.

There is nothing more important to the Christian life than the cultivation of good habits. The Bible is filled with instructions as to the right way to think and the right way to conduct life.

When we think of bad habits, we Christians often think first of smoking, drinking, and drugs. This series will include some reference to these extremely dangerous habits that beckon young people, but they will be considered within a broad range of habits that may be present in your youth group.

The goal of this four week study of habits is change. In a very real way, your teens will provide the direction that the sessions take. It will be up to them to identify the habits they wish to break and the habits they wish to establish. Your goal as a leader will be to help them identify those habits they most wish to change and to provide them with information, motivation, and support as they attempt to bring about lasting change.

Some say that it takes about a month and a half to make a new habit, while others suggest that if we maintain a certain behavior for three weeks we may well have it incorporated into our habit system. The effectiveness of this series may not be known during these four sessions, but it is hoped that they will provide incentive to begin a process that will lead to lasting change in their lives.

Session One is given over to the process of identifying habits, both good and bad. The purpose is to introduce the topic of habits and to lead young people to think deeply of the important role they play in defining, limiting, directing, and enabling their lives. It suggests that teens examine their lives and set some goals for change.

Session Two looks at bad habits and encourages teens to recognize that they need correction. It provides some guidelines for the breaking of undesirable habits.

Session Three concentrates on some dangerous habits that often lead to teenage addiction—drinking, smoking, drugs.

Session Four seeks to lead young people to establish disciplines and habits that will result in a Christian life-style. It concentrates on good habits and encourages them to begin the process of establishing them firmly in their lives. It includes a time of assessment, a time of commitment.

It is hard to imagine a series more important to the life-styles of young people than this. Pray earnestly that God will use these sessions to bring about lasting results that can be seen in holiness and righteousness.

This series should be particularly helpful as a diagnostic tool for the observant leader. Since the sessions are designed to include a great deal of thinking, teens should reveal to the leader many areas for future discussion and study. For example, if a number of teens list a "quiet time" as a habit that they wish to establish, the leader may want to follow this series with some specific teaching on the importance and nature of a daily devotional time. The problems that are identified in the course of these sessions should provide great insight into the needed direction for future study for your young people. Be alert to identify them as the sessions unfold.

PROJECT/ACTIVITY

This unit lends itself to quite a number of possible projects. At the beginning of the unit, meet with some of the most influential and creative teen leaders to brainstorm possible ideas for involvement learning. Here are a list of thoughts that might get you and your group started.

* A **Parent/Teen Evening** that might include some of the following:
1. A special speaker on the subject of teen problems (perhaps a local judge, probation officer, prosecutor, state patrolman, sheriff, or police officer).
2. A panel made up of a few parents and a few students to discuss a topic of interest to both. Perhaps parents could speak on the topic, "What Parents Wish Their Teens Understood About Parents" with the teens addressing themselves to the topic, "What Teens Wish Their Parents Understood About Teens."
3. A film series such as James Dobson's *Focus on the Family.*
4. A Christian counselor speaking on the topic: "Teen Habits That Lead to Adult Problems."
5. A panel of teens discussing the topic: "Things I Admire Most in People."
* A **fact and experience gathering project** that might include sending teens in groups or individually out to interview various people in your community. They should take tape recorders to transcribe their interviews and then write up brief reports to summarize what they learn.

There are a number of ways these interviews could be used. The easiest would be for teens to write up brief summaries of their findings and share them with the entire youth group. If you have someone in your church who is gifted in media things, the interview tapes might be edited and mixed in such a way as to create an interesting audio tape, using the voices of the interviewees themselves for the content. To take this one step further, a multi-media slide presentation might be put together with the tape for an interesting presentation on "The Most Important Things in Life."

* This unit lends itself very well to the use of **special speakers.** Check out the local law enforcement agencies to see what special speakers and educational materials they may have on teen problems such as drugs or drinking. Check out groups like Alcoholics Anonymous, Alanon, Gamblers Anonymous, Mothers Against Drunk Driving, or Students Against Drunk Driving to see if they have any representatives that could talk to teens about their organization.

* A **field trip** to a penitentiary, prison, jail, or other correctional facility might lead to good discussion of habits that harm. A field trip to an athletic training camp might lead to discussion of good health habits. A field trip to a college could lead to a discussion of good study habits. A field trip to a childrens home might lead to discussion of habits that build good families or wreck them.

These are just a few ideas. Your group can probably come up with many of their own. You might invite local self-help groups in to tell of their programs and distribute literature. You could use movies that speak to the question of values and life-style, such as *Chariots of Fire*. You could have VCR movies and programs that present material connected with life-style, habits, addictions, and Christian conduct.

Your group can create a fine program that will involve them in communicating to one another and to others some basic concepts relating to this unit.

ResouRces anD iDeas

Invite some special speakers to share with the group during the course of these sessions. A speaker from a local chapter of Alcoholics Anonymous could well bring special insights into the overcoming of alcohol. There may also be available a speaker from Gamblers Anonymous or Smokers Anonymous. Perhaps there

are county health services that work with people who desire to quit various habits. When a speaker comes, encourage the teens to look for keys into the conquering of their own bad habits. Warn them that they may disagree with some things the speaker may say, but that there is something to be learned from their experience in overcoming difficult habits. A representative of or participant in Weight Watchers might also give helpful information. Perhaps there is an adult in the congregation who has successfully overcome a troublesome habit and would be willing to share with the young people his or her experience.

There do not seem to be a great number of helpful books treating habits from a Christian perspective. *How to Say No to a Stubborn Habit* by Erwin W. Lutzer (Wheaton, IL: Scripture Press, Victor Books, 1979, $4.95) has some helpful information, as do two books by Rick Yohn, *Getting Control of Your Life* (Nashville, TN: Thomas Nelson Publishers, 1983, $4.95) and *Getting Control of Your Inner Self* (Wheaton, IL: Tyndale House Publishing, 1982, $2.95). Ward Patterson's book, *Triumph Over Temptation*, (Cincinnati, OH: Standard Publishing, 1984, $2.95), while not dealing directly with habits as such, does give background on the nature of temptation and insights into its overcoming. Many have found Richard J. Foster's book, *Celebration of Discipline* (New York, NY: Harper and Row, 1978, $10.95) to be very helpful in its practical advice concerning Christian disciplines. You may not agree with everything Foster writes, but the book is a fine encouragement to the establishment of habits of holiness.

1. SADD (Students Against Drunk Driving), 110 Pleasant Street, Marlborough, MA 01752 (617) 481-3568.
2. MADD (Mothers Against Drunk Driving), 669 Airport Freeway, Suite 310, Hurst, TX 760533 (817) 268-MADD.
3. CADD (Citizens Against Drunk Driving), Box 530, Schenectady, NY 12301 (518) 372-0034.
4. RID (Remove Intoxicated Drivers), Box 520, Schenectady, NY 12301 (518) 372-0034.
5. National Clearinghouse for Alcohol Information, Box 2345, Rockville, MD 20852.
6. American Cancer Society, 777 Third Avenue, NY 10017.

Session 1

YOU AND YOUR HABITS

OBJECTIVES

As a result of this session, teens should be able to do one or more of the following:

1. Identify five habits common to their own behavior and to the behavior of a friend or member of their family.
2. Construct a working definition of the word "habit."
3. List five things that contribute to the formation of our habits.
4. Differentiate between good habits and bad habits.
5. Evaluate present habits in their lives.

ADVANCE PREPARATION

1. Make copies of Worksheets 1-3 from the masters at the end of this unit.
2. Have one 3 x 5 card for everyone present.
3. Have plenty of Bibles, paper, and pencils available for use.

MEETING SCHEDULE

Ready	10 minutes
Research	20 minutes
Respond	25 minutes
Closing	5 minutes

READY

In order to introduce the topic that will be studied in this and the following three sessions, begin by reading the following.

WHAT IS MY NAME?

"You hear me when people talk. Some people call it an accent, but it's just me in one of my many forms. Some people call it etiquette, but it's just me in one of my other disguises. I help you walk without having to think about lifting your feet. I am your favorite color, your favorite cookie, your favorite hobby. I have been called the machinery of living. I may be a rut, or a life-style, or a tradition, or a skill. I am a basic tool of living. Sometimes I come quickly and sometimes I come very slowly. I am everywhere. I hit home runs and perform great symphonies. I destroy homes and break relationships. I kill some people and I free others. I bring people close to God and I lead them away from Him. I am created from repetitions. I am capable of helping people in their highest accomplishments and I am capable of enslaving and destroying them. What is my name?"

Ask if any one can guess the name. After "habits" has been revealed, read the paragraph again. Allow time to think about what is being said.

Point out that it is the goal of this series to make teens aware of their habits and how they reflect their faith in Christ. Tell them that they will not only learn about good and bad habits, but also receive help in breaking some undesirable habits and establishing some good ones. It may be helpful if you share with the group one habit that you want to break and one habit that you want to establish during the next four sessions.

RESEARCH

SPOT THE HABITS

Have one teen read this account of one family's Sunday morning activities. Suggest that they take notes on a piece of paper of the habits they spot in the behavior of the family.

Sunday Morning with the Hathaways

Let's look in on a typical Christian family as they prepare for church on Sunday morning.

Mrs. Hathaway is the first one up. She puts on her housecoat and makes her way to the kitchen. She sets out some donuts, cereal, milk, and orange juice for whomever is interested. Around this house, Sunday breakfast is an "every man for himself" meal! She then begins food preparations for dinner after church.

The noise from the kitchen awakens Mr. Hathaway. He slowly gets out of bed and makes his way to the bathroom. He shaves, showers, and returns to the bedroom to get dressed.

Mrs. Hathaway takes a break from the kitchen to make sure everyone is up and going.

She stops by Susie's room and finds that she is already up and in the bathroom. She notices that Todd's door is still closed. She knocks on the door and calls, "Todd, it's time to get up!" There is no response. "Todd! Todd!" He mutters something to let her know that he is awake and she goes on. At her bedroom door, she meets Mr. Hathaway who is on his way to the kitchen. He goes on to the kitchen while she stays in the bedroom to get ready. After he sees that the coffee is on, he brings in the paper from the driveway. He returns to the kitchen, grabs a cup of coffee, and opens up the sports page.

Mrs. Hathaway, still in her housecoat, has finished combing her hair and checks on Todd who is still in bed. She warns him that he had better get up or he will be late. He complains, "Susie has been in the bathroom all morning! I'll never get in there!" Mrs. Hathaway calls to Susie,, "Hurry up, honey, so Todd can get ready, too." She comes back to the kitchen and continues her preparation for dinner. She tries to talk to Mr. Hathaway who is too engrossed in the paper to hear her. She hears Susie leave the bathroom but doesn't hear Todd get up. So, again, she goes to his room and tells him the bathroom is empty and time is running out. He gets up slowly and starts for the bathroom. Mrs. Hathaway returns to her bedroom to finish getting dressed.

Susie comes out to the kitchen. She says hello to her father who acknowledges her presence but keeps on reading. She fixes a glass of orange juice and a bowl of cereal.

Mrs. Hathaway returns to the kitchen dressed and ready to go. She continues her dinner preparations where she left off.

Mr. Hathaway sees that everyone is almost ready and decides he will go start the car. On his way out, he tells Todd to get moving or he will be late.

Susie brushes her teeth, picks up her Bible, and joins her father in the car. Mrs. Hathaway clears off the table and puts the dishes in the sink. She picks up her Bible and tells Todd to hurry because it's time to go and they will be late. She joins the others in the car. Todd grabs a donut on his way through the kitchen and hurries out the door. His mother notices that he doesn't have his Bible and sends him back for it. His father tells him to hurry.

Todd locks the door on his way out and jumps into the car. Mr. Hathaway backs the car out of the driveway and they are on the way to church.

DISCUSSION

Ask teens to mention the habits they spotted in the story. Note that it is by habits that we come to know each other and that it is in habits that people are differentiated. Point out that habits are a standardized pattern of learned behavior. Share the following thoughts with the group.

"Fiction writers know the importance of detailing habits in their characters so that we come to know their personalities. In this story, we see habits of routine, habits of choice, habits of speech, habits of personal preference.

"In a very real sense, we are our habits. Mannerisms, personal preferences, established patterns of behavior, unconscious activity, and conscious choice all reflect habits of thought and action that mark us just as distinctly as our fingerprints.

"Many crimes are solved due to the fact that crimes are linked to specific criminals by their distinctive modes of operation. Missing persons are tracked by means of their habits—what magazines they like, what places they enjoy, what hobbies they are devoted to, what interests they pursue. Our habits identify us and define us. It is extremely important that we build good habits into our lives if we are going to be the kind of people God wants us to be."

RESPOND

HABITS

Distribute Worksheets 1 and 2. Instruct teens to answer the questions found on the pages. Set a time limit of 8-10 minutes. Encourage teens to work quickly so that there will be ample time for discussion.

When the time is up, move on to the discussion activity.

DISCUSSION

Continue this session with a discussion of teens' answers. Be affirming as you listen to what they have to say. The purpose of this exercise is not to elicit any particular answer, but to challenge the teens to think for themselves. Since this series of sessions deals with making and breaking habits, you will want to give special attention to the definition of habits. The dictionary definition of habit includes "a disposition or a characteristic condition of mind of body; a thing done often or easily; custom; a pattern of action that is acquired and has become so automatic that it is difficult to break; a tendency to perform a certain action or behave a certain way; and an addiction such as a dependency on narcotics." In the course of these sessions, we may define it more particularly, but this definition will help to suggest the wide variety of human behavior that is covered by the idea of habit. It should be pointed out that the word habit does not appear in the King James version of the Bible. There are, however, some passages that refer to customary actions (Luke 2:42; 4:16; Acts 6:14; 21:21). Beyond this, the Bible is filled with urgencies that we conform our thoughts and actions to God's will. As this section comes to an end, carefully discuss the Scriptures found on Worksheet 3. If your group is large, you may want to break it down into small groups and assign one or two Scriptures to each group.

HERE'S ONE FOR THE ROAD

Ask teens to think of two bad habits they would like to break and two good ones that they would like to establish in their lives. Give them 3 x 5 cards and ask them during the coming week to write the two good habits and the two bad habits on the card and not to sign their names. Tell them that the cards will be collected at the beginning of the next session.

CLOSING

Ask teens to read the Scripture passages on Worksheet 3 during the coming week and to examine their lives in light of them. Ask them to think about the habits they have established and to dedicate themselves to personal growth during this study. Ask them to think of the habits of Jesus and how they are models for our lives. Close with prayer.

SESSION 2

BREAKING HABITS

OBJECTIVES

As a result of this session, teens should be able to do one or more of the following:

1. Identify two bad habits in their lives which they would like to see broken.

2. List at least five principles that are of help in trying to break a bad habit.

3. Commit themselves, with God's help, to the breaking of one personal habit.

ADVANCE PREPARATION

1. Make a copy of Transparency A from the master at the end of this unit.

2. Have enough 3 x 5 cards for everyone.

3. Acquaint yourself thoroughly with the lecture material.

MEETING SCHEDULE

Ready	10 minutes
Research	25 minutes
Respond	20 minutes
Closing	5 minutes

READY

At the close of the last session, you gave out 3 x 5 cards and asked teens to list on them two habits they wished to make and two they wished to break. Ask one teen to collect these cards from the others. If some were not present last week or have forgotten their cards, give them cards and ask them to do the assignment as the session begins.

Ask one teen to list on one side of the chalkboard all the "wish to make" habits. On the other side, list all the "wish to break" habits. Give each of the teens another 3 x 5 card and ask each person to write down both lists.

Explain to the group that you would like for them to pray each day during the coming weeks that those who have listed these things might be successful. Tell them that it is not important that they know which person is dealing with what problem, but it is important that they pray for God's leading and help in the lives of their friends. Have a time of silent prayer as each teen prays for God's help in the habits listed. Close this prayer yourself, seeking God's assistance in the particular matters which have been shared.

RESEARCH

BUZZ GROUPS

Divide the teens into small groups of five or six each. On a 3 x 5 card, write one of the "wish to break" habits for each small group. Give this card to one member of a group and ask that person to role play as if that is a habit he or she wishes to break. Describe the situation in this way: "The person with the card has come to your group for advice. He or she wants to break the habit that is on the card. The task of the group is to come up with a list of things that will help this person break the unwanted habit. The person who has the 'habit card' should take seriously his or her role. He or she should dialogue with the group in a manner that represents a real person with that habit to break. The group should treat the person with the 'habit card' as a real person who has come to the small group for personal advice."

When the groups clearly understand the situation, ask one other person in each group to serve as a recorder. The recorder's task is to write down in a brief form the main points of the advice that the group gives to the "habit breaker." Acknowledge that there is a place for humor, but emphasize that the task of the groups is very important. The habit they are dealing with is important to at least one member of the group and it ought not to be trivialized. The purpose of the exercise is to give them practice in counseling one another. Emphasize that it is important that they be helpful and specific in their counsel. Encourage each member to take part in the discussion. Tell them that they will have eight minutes to come up with their proposals for change.

As the groups work, create other habit cards from the master list. When time is called, give a new habit card to a new group member who will become the "habit breaker" for the next eight minute segment. Ask another person in each group to serve as recorder. Adjust this exercise according to the size and nature of groups and the number of "habits to break" on your master list.

RESPOND

Ask the recorders to share with everyone the advice given by their groups in the "habit breakers." Have one come to the chalkboard and write the name of the habit. In a column below the habit, list the advice given by the small group in relation to that habit. Go through all the habits without great elaboration or comment.

When this task has been finished, see if you can summarize the advice given into a number of steps that are common to all of the habits. List these under the title: "Habit-Breaking Principles."

LECTURE

The material that follows is designed to make some specific suggestions as to the breaking of habits. Many of the things discussed may already have been suggested by the group. If so, recognize that fact as you share this material. Try to feature the thoughts of the group as you summarize and add some ideas that they may not have mentioned. Share the following thoughts with the group.

"Raise your hands if you have ever made New Year's resolutions. Have you ever been successful in keeping the resolutions? Why does it seem that we break our good resolutions so quickly? Breaking habits is big business. From "fat farms" to alcoholic rehabilitation centers to Weight Watchers to marriage counselors to self-improvement seminars to hypnotism to acupuncture, people are constantly seeking ways to bring undesirable habits under control. Behavior modification is an "in" topic in psychology. Countless cults and self-help courses promise freedom and power over self and others. All of us have habits which we have failed to break. Some of them are little more than individual idiosyncrasies. Others are major areas of weakness and sin. It is our prayer that we may take on some major area of weakness during these next few weeks. Then we may rejoice in God's blessing of freedom in your life. The things we will mention are not magic formulas. Some of the suggestions will apply better to some habits than to others. Not all undesirable habits are alike and they must be approached differently. It is our purpose, however, to present some suggestions that may be useful in your approach to undesirable habits.

"Richard Stiller, in his book, *Habits*, (Cornerstone, 1980), lists six basic habit-breaking approaches he says are suggested by people who are successful habit breakers:

1. Create a new and competing habit to take the place of the old.
2. "Wear out" the old habit—force the person to repeat it over and over again until disgust and/or exhaustion takes over and weakens its hold.
3. Associate the bad habit with an unpleasant experience or sensation.
4. If the habit is a phobia, gradually expose the person to small, nonthreatening experiences until the feared experience is no longer so frightening.
5. Interrupt the sequence of the habit, or change the setting in which it is usually triggered in order to disrupt the patterns and pathways.
6. Punishment. James L. Mursell, in his book, *How to Make and Break Habits,* asserts that habits grow because they offer a measure of satisfaction. He says, "Bad habits, inadequate habits, disastrous habits persist simply and solely because they are the only ways of dealing with a problem that a person can see, the only tools that seem available" (p. 83). Part of the changing of a habit is to find some other, more beneficial way of dealing with a problem and finding satisfaction. Here then are some things to consider in approaching a troublesome habit:

1. *Admit to yourself that the habit you want to change is really harmful.* You must not try to excuse it by saying, "Oh, that's just the way I am." You must call it for what it is, particularly if it is a habit that is contrary to God's revealed will for your life.

2. *Be honest with yourself.* Do *you* really want to change? Do you really think that change is desirable for you? Are you convinced that your life will be better if you kick your habit?

3. *Take personal responsibility for your habits.* Don't blame them on circumstances or other people. Recognize that you have the ability and power, with God's help, to overcome them.

4. *Ask God to assist you in reaching your goal.* James wrote, "The prayer of a righteous man is powerful and effective" (James 5:16b, NIV). Ask God to give you the will and the ability to break from the bondage of the undesirable habit.

5. *On a regular basis read Scriptures that emphasize God's power at work in your life.* Memorize Scriptures that encourage you to better living and speak of victory through Christ. Examples of such Scriptures are: 1 John 5:4; 1 Peter 2:11, 12; Ephesians 3:20, 21; Ephesians 4:22-32; 1 Corinthians 9:26, 27; Hebrews 6:12; 2 Corinthians 6:16; 1 Corinthians 6:19.

6. *Examine the habit carefully.* Is it a symptom of some other problem area in your life? Do you, for instance, cut people down in your speech because you do not feel accepted by others? Is your habit the real problem or is it a symptom of another problem that needs to be addressed? See if you can identify the base problem and begin working on it.

7. *Seek the assistance, support, and encouragement of others.* James says, "Therefore confess your sins to each other and pray for each other so that you may be healed." (James 5:16a). It is important that we have someone to pray with us, hold us accountable, and encourage us. This may be a good friend in whom you can confide your desire to kick a particular habit. This person will need to hold up your goals before you, to confront you when you feel like quitting in your struggle, and rejoice with you in your progress. Groups like Alcoholics Anonymous and Weight Watchers know the benefits to be found in having others who are rooting for us.

8. *Set some specific goals.* Set realistic goals for yourself. The psychologist, William James, said that it takes at least 45 days to break a habit. Others suggest about three weeks of changed behavior will serve to free us from many unwanted habits. Set some measurable goals and rejoice as you see them accomplished.

9. *Be willing to seek professional help.* In matters such as drug addiction, alcoholism, homo-

sexuality, and chronic gambling, there are centers, counselors, programs, and groups ready to give help. Avail yourself of those programs that are consistent with Christian faith in their approach to your problem.

10. *Keep in mind the reason you want to change the behavior.* If you are working on overeating, for instance, you ought to install a full length mirror in a place where you can't escape it. If you are quitting smoking, you might want to tape some facts about lung cancer in a place where you frequently see them. Remember, however, that your purpose is not primarily self improvement, it is to live a life that is pleasing to God.

11. *Visualize yourself as you will be when you have conquered your undesirable habit.* We welcome what we believe ourselves to be. Rather than focusing on the habit itself, focus on the desired benefits the change will bring about in your life.

12. *Fill the vacuum left by the abolition of the bad habit with a good habit.* Romans 12:21 says, "Do not be overcome by evil, but overcome evil with good" *(NIV).*

A bad habit is often the flip side of a good habit. What we are learning as we break a habit is actually the formation of another habit that is beneficial.

13. *Examine the habit to see what its components are.* What things set the scene for the habit you are trying to break? Can you avoid the familiar setting that leads to your indulging the undesirable habit. Do you need to break a relationship with people who encourage you to continue in your undesirable habit? Can you avoid the temptation to do it by avoiding certain places or persons?

14. *Learn from others who have overcome the habit you are working on.* Often the best instructor you can have is a person who has found victory in the area that troubles you. If you have bad study habits, find a person with good study habits and allow that person to instruct you.

15. *Do not give up if you have a temporary lapse.* Remember that the habit has had some time to take hold of you. Realize that it may take some time for you to break free. Don't give up if you fail. Begin again, and again if necessary. Don't allow Satan to convince you that

you are powerless. A lapse may be a temporary setback, but it need not be a defeat, unless you allow it to be.

16. *Be careful of pride once you have licked the habit.* Those who work with alcoholics note that sometimes a person will seek help when he is down and out. Once the person begins to dry out, things in his life begin to go better. He gains confidence in himself and sees the beneficial results of his changed life. Then he may feel that he is strong enough to handle alcohol again. This leads to a return to drink and a rapid skid back to the depths from which he came. We may overcome some habits easily, but others may be persistent temptations for us. In the latter case, we must recognize that we are always vulnerable to return to our former habits.

HERE'S ONE FOR THE ROAD

Ask each teen to choose one of the two bad habits listed on the 3 x 5 cards they brought with them today and to pray to God about breaking it. Encourage them to put the principles talked of today into practice. Ask them to take this assignment seriously so that the whole group can rejoice and thank God for the changes that will come. Encourage anyone who wishes to talk about the habit he has chosen to break. If you feel comfortable doing so, share with the group the habit you yourself have chosen to overcome. Let them know how you have begun to apply the above guidelines and principles to your own life.

CLOSING

Thank teens for their serious attention and for their contributions to the discussion. Encourage them to pray for God's help in their quest for freedom from the bondage of bad habits. Close the session with prayer.

Session 3

ADDICTIVE HABITS

YOU CAN'T EAT JUST ONE.

CHIP

CHIPS CHIPS CHIPS CHIPS

OBJECTIVES

As a result of this session, teens should be able to do one or more of the following:

1. Describe the real effects of drinking, gambling, smoking, or taking drugs and how they are different than the way they are presented from people who have a vested interest in hooking others on the habit.

2. Identify four spiritual or health hazards related to each of the habits discussed in this session.

ADVANCE PREPARATION

1. Make copies of the *IVI Reports* script for all the participants from the master at the end of this unit.

2. Assign the parts for the *IVI Reports* to interested teens. There are 5 speaking parts (Chairman of the Board, Mr. Al Cohol, Ms. Gay Ming, Mr. Nick O'Teen, and Ms. Mary Wana) and 2 silent parts (the men who remove Mr. Nick O'Teen from the room). Give the scripts to the young people so they can learn their parts and rehearse the skit sometime before the session.

3. The *IVI Reports* relate a lot of statistical information. You may want to have some interested teens design some visuals (posters, flip charts or transparencies) to help illustrate the information.

4. Prepare a stage area in the room. The setting should include an oblong table with a chair at each end and three on the side facing the audience.

5. Have a Bible concordance and a topical Bible ready for use.

6. Have plenty of Bibles, paper, envelopes, and pencils available for use.

MEETING SCHEDULE	
Ready	5 minutes
Research	30 minutes
Respond	20 minutes
Closing	5 minutes

READY

As teens arrive, explain to them that this session will deal with some habits which are extremely dangerous and can become extremely harmful addictions.

Explain to them that the habits for discussion will be introduced by means of a reader theater. They are to imagine that the table before them is in a very plush board room of a successful corporation. Explain that while the actors will be reading their lines, the audience is to imagine them as real actors in a play. Make sure everyone has a pencil and paper. Explain to them that at the end of the play they will be given time to write a paragraph on one of the discussed habits. They should explain how its reality is different from the way it is presented to us by those who have a vested interested in our becoming hooked.

Research

The IVI Reports

Have the actors present the play, *The IVI Reports* at this time. Encourage others to give their full attention during the performance.

Respond

At the conclusion of the play, ask teens to write a paragraph on the difference between illusion and reality in one of the four habit areas. Assign a habit to each teen, making sure that someone in the group will be writing about each of them. Tell them that they will be given only four minutes to work, so they must move quickly. At the end of the allotted time, ask as many teens as possible to read their paragraphs to the group. Elaborate on the things they say and point out the special insights that are brought to the discussion.

Hazard Hunt

Ask teens to list on a sheet of paper at least four spiritual or health hazards related to each of the four habits discussed in the *IVI Reports* — drinking, smoking, gambling, drugs. Give them about six minutes to prepare their lists, then ask them to share their thoughts with the group. You may want to note their thoughts on a blackboard using key words.

Here's One For The Road

Give each teen an envelope and two sheets of paper. Ask each one if he or she has any friends who are taking up any of the habits we have talked about today. Ask them to imagine that they are writing a letter to such a friend to encourage him or her not to continue. They will want to point out the dangers of the habit and refer to Biblical passages that the friend ought to take into consideration. Encourage them to do individual research and be as persuasive as possible. Call their attention to concordances and Bible helps that will assist them. Encourage them also to get the thoughts of their parents or of another strong Christian they know.

If time permits, have them start this project during the meeting time. Tell them to be sure to finish their work during the week and to bring their letters with them to the next session.

Explain that this session has been on habits that a Christian should avoid. Next week we will consider some habits that a Christian should seek to develop.

Closing

Point out that the facts and statistics in the *IVI Reports* indicate wide acceptance of the harmful habits discussed in today's session. This should never influence us to accept them. We, as Christians, must be willing to be different from the majority in many areas of our lives. We are set apart to God and our life-styles must reflect our Christian values. Our bodies are the temples of the Holy Spirit (See 1 Corinthians 3:16, 17; 6:19, 20; 2 Corinthians 6:14-18). They are to be treated with respect and care. We are not to seek our satisfaction from a bottle or a pill. Rather, we are to find out satisfaction in the things of God. The addictions we have studied today give short range "highs" but their final effect is disease, heartbreak, and ruin. Paul wrote to the Ephesians, "Do not get drunk on wine, which leads to debauchery. Instead be filled with the Spirit" (5:18). God intends to give us, through His Spirit, true happiness, not the fake highs of addicting drink and drugs. Close with prayer.

Session 4

Making Habits

Objectives

As a result of this session, teens should be able to do one or more of the following:

1. Identify five habits that a Christian should strive to establish in his or her life.

2. Prepare a plan by which good habits can be incorporated into a Christian life-style.

3. Set personal goals leading to the establishment of a new desirable habit.

Advance Preparation

1. Make copies of Worksheet 4 from the master at the end of this unit.

2. Remind several of your group members that they will need to complete their letters that were assigned in the last session. These will be used as a part of the *Ready* activity.

3. Locate the article, "And Not So Sudden Death," by Robert J. White in the July 1983 issue of *Readers Digest,* pages 96-100 (check the public library).

4. Be sure there are plenty of Bibles, 3 x 5 cards, and pencils available for use.

Meeting Schedule

Ready	10 minutes
Research	15 minutes
Respond	30 minutes
Closing	5 minutes

Ready

Open the session by having someone read the article "And Not So Sudden Death" to the group. Explain that, in a way, this article is a letter from a neurosurgeon to young people. Then ask some teens to share with the group the letters they were asked to begin at the close of the last session. Explain that they may or may not really send these letters to friends, but that they are an exercise to help them explain their beliefs about the dangerous habits of drinking, gambling, smoking, and drugs.

Discuss briefly the main points that teens make in their letters. Try to read at least one on each of the four habits.

Explain to them that it is not only important to break bad habits. It is also important to establish good habits and good Christian disciplines in our lives.

RESEARCH

SCRIPTURE STUDY

There are six chapters in 1 Timothy, four in 2 Timothy, and five in James. Depending on the number of 5 person groups that you can create, assign one, two, or three of these books. Assign a chapter to each small group. Ask each group to appoint a scribe who will record what the group says. The task for each group is to identify the good habits and the bad habits that are mentioned or suggested in each chapter. Ask the scribe to make notes in two columns as key words are mentioned. Here is a list of nouns, verbs, and adjectives describing desirable and undesirable habits:

1 Timothy

Chapter 1
BAD: spreading falsehood; empty speculation; controversy; meaningless talk; ignorant arrogance; lawbreaking; rebellion; ungodliness; sinfulness; unholiness; irreligion; murder; adultery; perversion; slavery; lying; falsehood; blasphemy; violence; ignorance; unbelief.
GOOD: love; pure heart; good conscience; sincere faith; mercy.

Chapter 2
BAD: anger, disputing; extravagance; ostentation.
GOOD: patience; prayer; godliness; holiness; peace; modesty; good deeds; submission; faith; love; holiness.

Chapter 3
BAD: drinking of much wine; violence; quarrelsomeness; greed; conceit.
GOOD: Above reproach; faithfulness in marriage; temperance; self-control; respectableness; hospitality; able to teach; gentleness; good management; good parent; good reputation; sincere; honest; faithful; respectable, trustworthy; temperate; good manager; service.

Chapter 4
BAD: lying; hypocrisy; godlessness.
GOOD: thanksgiving; belief; prayer; godliness; hope; belief; good example in speech, life, love, faith, and purity; reading of Scripture; preaching; teaching; using spiritual gift; diligency; circumspectness; perseverance.

Chapter 5
BAD: harsh rebuke; denying the faith; sensual desires; broken pledges; idleness; busybodies; gossip; unbelief; partiality; favoritism.
GOOD: exhortation; kindness; purity; recognition; caring; pray; seeking God's help; faithful to marriage; good deeds; loving toward children; hospitality; caring; helping; good deeds; belief; responsibility; preaching; teaching; discipline; impartiality; good deeds.

Chapter 6
BAD: slander; false doctrine; conceit; ignorance; controversy; argument; envy; quarreling; malicious talk; evil suspicions; constant friction; greed; corruption; foolish desires; love of money; departure from faith; hope in riches.
GOOD: respect; service; godliness; contentment; righteousness; godliness; faith; love; endurance; gentleness; steadfastness; obedience; humility; hope in God; joy; good deeds; generosity; sharing; diligence; shun evil.

2 Timothy

Chapter 1
GOOD: prayer; joy; faith; power; love; self-discipline; suffering for gospel; holy living; conviction; sound teaching; unashamed loyalty.

Chapter 2
BAD: disowning Christ; faithlessness; quarreling; godless chatter; apostasy; wickedness; evil desires; foolish arguments; quarrels; resentment.
GOOD: strength; teach; endurance; resoluteness; diligence; remembrance; truth; confession; cleansing ourselves; noble purpose;

holiness; good work; righteousness; faith; love; peace; purity of heart; prayer; kindness; able to teach; gentleness; repentance.

Chapter 3
BAD: self love; love of money; boasting; pride; abusiveness; disobedience; ingratitude; unholiness; unloving; treachery; rash action; conceit; pleasure lovers; denying power of godliness; sin; evil desires; not recognizing truth; opposition to truth; depraved mind; rejecting faith; foolishness; deceitfulness.
GOOD: faith; patience; love; endurance; persecution; suffering; godliness; wisdom; conviction; teaching; rebuking; correcting; training in righteousness; good work.

Chapter 4
BAD: closed to sound doctrine; calloused; apostasy; love of world; desertion; opposition of God's people; evil attack.
GOOD: preach; be prepared; correct; rebuke; calm; endurance; evangelize; minister; sacrifice; resoluteness; endurance; loyalty; help; strength.

James

Chapter 1
BAD: instability; pride; evil desire; enticement; sin.
GOOD: joy; faith; perseverance; maturity; wisdom; prayer; unbelief; resoluteness; humility; perseverance; love; quick to listen; slow to speak; slow to anger; clean life; humility; act on word; obedience; control of tongue; purity; faultlessness; service; purity.

Chapter 2
BAD: favoritism; discrimination; evil thoughts; sin; lawbreaking; merciless judgment.
GOOD: love; clear-sightedness; mercy; faith; faithful action; good deeds; righteousness.

Chapter 3
BAD: corrupt tongue; cursing; bitter envy; selfish ambition; boasting; denying truth; un-

spiritual wisdom; envy; selfish ambition; disorder; evil deeds.
GOOD: praise; wisdom; understanding; good life; humility; purity; peace loving; consideration; submissiveness; merciful; fruitfulness; impartiality; sincerity; peace; righteousness.

Chapter 4
BAD: quarreling; battles; greed; murder; covetousness; fighting; bad motives; selfish pleasure; friendship of the world; hatred of God; friendship with world; enemy of God; envy; pride; slander; harsh judgment; boasting.
GOOD: prayer; grace; submission; seeking God; cleansing; purity repentance; humility; trust.

Chapter 5
BAD: hoarding wealth; fraud; self-indulgence; condemnation; murder; grumbling.
GOOD: patience, firmness; perseverance; compassion; mercy; unadorned truth; prayer; praise; faith; confession; concern for others.

RESPOND

Choose one or more of the following activities to continue this session.

1. Discussion
When the groups have finished their assigned task, ask each scribe to read briefly the bad and good habits mentioned or alluded to in the assigned chapter.

2. Honing In
Ask the groups to choose one of the good Christian characteristics mentioned and consider the habits that go into making it a part of their lives. To spur them on in this discussion, distribute Worksheet 4. Let them use the questions on the worksheet to guide their thoughts.

For the leader's benefit, here is a list of specific topics you might suggest for each group, according to the chapters they studied:

1 Timothy	1—Love
	2—Submission
	3—Good management
	4—Prayer
	5—Purity
	6—Generosity
2 Timothy	1—Self-discipline
	2—Kindness
	3—Wisdom
	4—Evangelism
James	1—Control of Tongue
	2—Good Deeds
	3—Praise
	4—Humility
	5—Compassion

Be sure that each group has a scribe that is taking notes and will be prepared to share with the larger group the thinking of the small group. Give them about ten minutes for small group discussion, then assemble into a large group again and share the thinking of the groups on the habits they have discussed.

3. Delaying Improvement

Discuss with teens why and how we often put off dealing with habits in our lives. Such things as the following may be mentioned:

1. Because we never really get started.
2. Because we set our goals too high and we just cannot reach them.
3. Because we allow our old habits to prevail before the new are established.
4. Because we give up before the new habit is firmly established.
5. Because we don't think we have the time to continue.
6. Because we miss something that the bad habit gave us.
7. Because we don't really pray consistently about it.
8. Because we are not patient enough to accomplish change.
9. Because of pressure from friends who want us to return to old ways.
10. Because we don't want to pay the cost in terms of discipline and regularity.

Encourage young people to work alone now and to have a time of silent prayer and meditation. Ask them to set a strategy for establishing one of the good Christian habits that have been discussed today. Ask them to look at the bottom of Worksheet 4 and complete the sentences. The sentences appear as follows:

1. I intend to . . .
2. I think it is important for me to do this because . . .
3. I will start . . .
4. In order to do this, I will need to . . .
5. When I establish this habit, I will be a better person because . . .

Encourage them to pray deeply, to ask God to enable them to do what they desire, and that they will have the commitment to continue until this good habit becomes a permanent part of their life-styles. Encourage them also to find within the youth group at least one person with whom they can share their goals and who will pray with them and hold them accountable to those goals.

Impress upon them the importance of good habits of thought, mind, and action to the Christian life.

4. Habit Hopper

Mention that we are now coming to the end of this unit on habits, but that there is still a lot more to say about the good habits and disciplines that should be developed in the Christian life. We have studied a lot about habits in general and have tried to help them think about the habits that go together to make their life-styles. It would be useful, as a next step, to know what are their areas of struggle and what are their goals. Give each person a 3 x 5 card and ask him or her to list one good habit and one bad habit that would merit further teaching. Ask them not to sign these cards, but to give them to you as they leave the session. These topics might help you to chart some of the future Bible teaching for your youth group.

Closing

Point out to the group that in a discussion like this, it is very easy to become discouraged when we compare our attitudes, actions, and priorities to those we know we ought to have as Christians. Point out to them that the Holy Spirit is given to the Christians as an encourager and enabler. (Galatians 5:16-26; 2 Peter 1:2-7; Romans 8:11-14; Philippians 2:13). Close with prayer.

HaBiTS

1. List five of your habits.

2. List five habits you have observed in a friend or family member.

3. Complete this definition

   "A habit is ... "

4. List some of the habits the laws of our land impose on us.

5. List three reasons you believe that habits benefit us.

6. List five things you would call your good habits.

7. List five things you would call your bad habits.

8. If you wanted to establish a new good habit, how would you go about it?

9. If you wanted to break a bad habit, how would you go about it?

10. Have you ever had success in breaking a bad habit? If so, how did you break it?

How could you relate the following Scripture to the subject of habits?

1. Romans 12:1, 2

2. Romans 12:21

3. Ephesians 3:16-19

4. Ephesians 4:29-34

5. Ephesians 5:1-7

6. Ephesians 5:15-21

7. 1 Timothy 4:12-16

8. 1 Timothy 6:17-21

9. 2 Timothy 2:22-26

10. 1 Thessalonians 4:3-12

DiSCUSSiON QUESTiONS

1. What does the Bible say about the importance of this habit?

2. What is involved in the establishing of this habit?

3. What are the benefits of firmly establishing this habit in our lives?

4. What will be the consequences if we fail to establish this habit firmly in our lives?

5. What are some possible components of the habit?

6. What would a person want to do who wished to make this element a habit of life?

7. How would the group suggest a person begin if he wished to establish this habit during the next three months?

PERSONaL GOaL SETTiNG

1. I intend to . . .

2. I think it is important because . . .

3. I will start . . .

4. In order to do this, I will need to . . .

5. When I establish this new habit, I will be a better person because . . .

HABIT-BREAKING PRINCIPLES

1. Admit to yourself that the habit you want to change is really harmful.

2. Be honest with yourself.

3. Take personal responsibility for your habits.

4. Ask God to assist you in reaching your goal.

5. On a regular basis, read Scriptures that emphasize God's power at work in your life.

6. Examine the habit carefully.

7. Seek the assistance, support, and encouragement of others.

8. Set some specific goals.

9. Be willing to seek professional help.

10. Keep in mind the reason you want to change the behavior.

11. Visualize yourself as you will be when you have conquered your undesirable habit.

12. Fill the vacuum left by the abolition of the bad habit with a good habit.

13. Examine the habit to see what its components are.

14. Learn from others who have overcome the habit you are working on.

15. Do not give up if you have a temporary lapse.

16. Be careful of pride once you have licked the habit.

THE I.V.I. REPORTS

(Chairman sits at the head of the table, stage right. The other four sit around the table so that they can rise to read reports as if to the CHAIRMAN. The students can read their reports as if from a manuscript, but the lines should be placed in such a way that they seem real and spontaneous.)

CHAIRMAN OF THE BOARD *(rising to his feet):* We are very glad to welcome you to our annual meeting of Division Directors. I believe you all know one another. On my left is Ms. Mary Wanna, vice-president in charge of our Pharmacology Division. Next to her is Mr. Al Cohol of our Beverage Division. Then, Mr. Nick O'Teen of our Fashion Division, and Ms. Gay Ming of our Sports Accessories Division. As you all know, this as been a dream year for Illusion Vendors Incorporated. Our illusions have made the newspapers almost daily. Our stock has never been higher. The products endorsed by IVI and bearing the IVI "Seal of Ap-

proval" are finding their way into nearly every home in the nation. And to you belongs the credit for IVI's phenomenal record. We are very proud of you. We enthusiastically acclaim your success and we eagerly await the activity reports of each of your divisions. We want you to share with us your problems, your successes, and your methods, and your plans for the future.

I think it is only fitting that we should start with Mr. Al Cohol. As you know, for the fifth consecutive year, Mr. Cohol has received the "National Ill-use Award" for his remarkable success with our beverage illusions. *(Chairman leads others in applauding. He sits down as Mr. Cohol rises.)*

MR. AL COHOL: Thank you for those kind words, Mr. Chairman. It has been another consummate year for the Beverage Division. The success of the Beverage Division however, is due to a cooperative effort of the whole IVI staff—advertisers, salesmen, manufacturers, and researchers.

I am happy to report that 96 million people in the United States use our product line. That is nearly two thirds of the adult population. Production levels have been up in recent years. In 1982 we produced 194 million barrels of beer, 96 million gallons of whiskey, and 576.4 million gallons of wine. We have succeeded in creating a captive market of about 10 million people. Some who do not look kindly upon our products describe these as "problem drinkers" and alcoholics. I rather like to think of them as extremely eager customers. When you think that these 10 million touch the lives of another 40 million people with the benefits of their addiction to our products, you can see why we are considered such an influential business.

Our products are responsible for tremendous benefits to our nation. It is estimated by the United States department of Health and Human Services that our products cost $50 billion a year in lost production, personal and property damage, motor vehicle accidents, fire losses, and health and medical costs. Just think what a spur we are to the American economy—all the cars we wreck, all the house we burn down, all the hospitals we fill, all the prisons we keep in business. Just think of all the divorce lawyers who owe us for their lucrative practices, all the social workers and ministers who are employed to deal with the situations we create, and all the undertakers who are benefited by our products.

We can take credit for half of all traffic fatalities, one third of all suicides, half of all fatal falls, half of all drownings, over half of all wife beatings, one third of all child abuse, half of all fire fatalities, and one third of all violent crimes. At least 650,000 people are sent to hospitals in alcohol-related accidents and 25,000

people die. Just to show how well we're doing, that means that there is a person killed every 21 minutes. We contribute to cirrhosis of the liver, heart disease, kidney and stomach disease, throat and mouth cancer, lowered resistance to infection, and serious mental disorders. Just think how much we contribute to the health industry by supplying them with customers! It is estimated that over 12 per cent of all national health expenditures are related to frequent and continual use of our products.

I am glad to inform you that we are increasingly an equal opportunity merchandiser. Forty years ago most women did not drink at all. Now I am happy to report that we have 60 per cent of them firmly committed to consume our products. Ninety per cent of college-age women drink. While the figure is most certainly higher now, in 1975 we could claim nearly a million women alcoholics. I must admit that this market has been set back somewhat by research findings that our products are extremely harmful to the unborn babies of expectant mothers who drink our products. Fetal Alcohol Syndrome is said to led to babies who have decreased heartbeats, are mentally retarded, and are deformed in the face, heart, and limbs. We are hopeful that this information will not be circulated widely and that those who learn of it will be so dependent on our products that they will be unable to do without them.

We believe in telling the world about the benefits our products bring. In 1980 we spent nearly $558 million on television, magazine, and newspaper advertising. Our advertising campaign is designed to convince the public that liquor is an aid to gracious living, a mark of hospitality, and a means of beneficial relaxation. Total alcoholic beverage sales is now over $59 billion a year. This is nearly six times the amount of money given to churches. In addition to our paid advertising, we receive a tremendous amount of free publicity from television. A California study has shown that the viewing public sees, on the average, eight drinking scenes an hour. It is estimated that the average young person sees 4000 drinking scenes a year on television. This must certainly explain our success with the young. We are assisted by the fact that 28 million children are the sons and daughters of alcoholics, but we can take justifiable credit for initiating the youth of our nation to consumption of our beverages at an increasingly early age. A good measure of our success is the fact that alcohol-related crashes are the leading cause of death in the 16-24 age group. Alcohol was found in the blood of over half of all teenage drivers killed in traffic accidents in 1980. Forty-three per cent had enough alcohol to be declared legally drunk. The American Red Cross reports that one in three high school students rides in a car driven by a heavy drinker at least once a month. While this is good news, I am sure that, we can do better. We cannot rest on our laurels even though over half of high school boys have drinking and driving problems. Only four out of ten high school girls can make the same claim.

We know that the future of our industry depends on our recruitment of the young. We spend a great deal for advertising in college newspapers. We sponsor athletic events for the young. We employ sports heroes to push our products. We are succeeding in our efforts to guarantee the future. A New York study found that half of the high school students in that area drank and that a third drank heavily at least once a week. Nearly 2 out of 10 had a serious alcohol dependency.

We hope to see great advances in our illusion during the coming year. Our beer division has been particularly successful with its low calorie products. Our liquor division continues to promote the theme of elegance and good breeding. We encourage "moderation," for we know that no one can become dependent on our products if he does not begin.

The success of the beverage illusion has been gratifying. This has largely been due to two factors: the design of our advertising campaign and the remarkable nature of our illusion itself. Our market researchers report that we have in this product a sure seller. If we induce the first drink, we are on our way. Moderation makes moderation more difficult. Some people experience the immediate benefits of alcoholism.

Most can drink for ten or twenty years before they develop the characteristics of a true alcoholic. The secret of our success is that we have a highly addicting liquid narcotic that is socially acceptable in our country. The sales appeal is practically irresistible. We are fortunate that we do not have to battle the discriminatory laws which hamper the Pharmacology Division so ably directed by Ms. Wana.

Before I conclude my report, I think it only fitting that I should express my gratitude to a group of customers who have been especially cooperative in making this another banner year for the Beverage Division and IVI. I would like to toast the millions of occasional and moderate drinkers for their marvelous work in making it possible for us to present our product in its most desirable light. By their help we enlist countless dependent users.

I could go on and on, but I see that I have already spoken longer than the time allotted to me. I would like to close with a little story put out by the OPPOSITION. Dr. Robert Moon says, "Suppose that there are one hundred and fifty million cows in America. Suppose a thriving industry is producing Old Scarecrow hay by aging it in the cornfield. Suppose this Old Scarecrow hay makes cows do strange things like running into barbed wire fences, jumping off bridges, running in front of automobiles and getting killed, and in cutting down in milk production fifty million gallons a year. Suppose that this Old Scarecrow hay is advertised on billboards in every pasture and is sold as the hay for cows of distinction, the hay that belongs, and the hay that makes social life more congenial. Suppose for every addict of Old Scarecrow hay cured, ten new addicts spring up in the barn. It would not be long until the farmers of America would say, 'Brothers, that ain't hay,' and banish it from the pasture."

Dr. Moon, with the usual naivete of the OPPOSITION, fails to see the real point. No, "it ain't hay." But it is the greatest illusion that has ever been on the market.

MR. CHAIRMAN: Thank you, Mr. Cohol. In your usual excessive manner you have taken more time than was allotted to you. But because of the great things you have to report, we shall forgive you once again. Now we should like to hear the news from our Sports Accessories Division under the capable direction of Ms. Gay Ming.

MS. GAY MING: It is difficult to follow such a competent speaker as Mr. Cohol. His reputation for illusion-manship is certainly well earned. We of Sports Accessories, however, also have encouraging news to report.

Again this year we have presented the buying public with a rather diversified line. We have stayed with the prosperous items of the past: cards, horses, dice, numbers, roulette, slot machine, bingo, and lotteries. We have been particularly successful in our new lottery promotions, with a number of states adopting our illusion as a regular feature for state revenue.

Gambling produces an annual turnover of at least $17 billion, a 340 per cent increase in the last fourteen years.

There are many unfair laws that still hamper us. Nevertheless, we have been able to hurdle them easily. Legality has never been a high priority for our division. We prefer more, shall I say, creative and individualistic approaches. A United States Attorney in New Jersey recognized our special nature when he said, "Gambling fosters crime, breeds crime, and finances crime." We, of course, argue that legalizing gambling removes it from the hands of the criminal element and secures its huge revenues for public benefit. We are doing our best to suppress a federal study that said, "There is no evidence that available legal games reduce illegal gambling.... Legal games may even increase illegal gambling by enticing additional bettors."

Even religious and charitable organizations are now handling our bingo and raffle line. This has been a great factor in the rising tide of acceptability our division is experiencing. Television networks feature odds makers as commentators. Nevada and New Jersey hotels draw people to their slot machines and gaming tables from all over the United States. Every year we achieve a rising level of legitimacy. We

continue to sharpen the "something for nothing" desire in American people.

Nearly 2/3 of adult Americans gamble in office pools, casinos, bingo games, horse and dog races, lotteries, jai lai, and off-track betting. A recent poll indicated that nearly 80 per cent of Americans approve of gambling in some form.

We have continued our friendship with law enforcement agencies and have found little hindrance there, despite the occasional run-in. While some would dare to call our business methods "corruption," I, however, like to think of them as "good aggressive business practice."

The number of compulsive gamblers has skyrocketed in the last few years as gambling has become more and more accessible to the masses. The number of our favorite gamblers, the compulsives, has grown from 4 million in 1976 to as many as 10 million today. Dr. Robert L. Custer, a Veterans Administration psychologist describes compulsive gambling as "One of the purest forms of psychological addictions know. Compulsive gamblers," he says, "are stimulated by gambling, get high on it, and have withdrawal symptoms when they stop." The compulsive may know that he has only one chance in 2,667 of hitting the jackpot on a slot machine. He may even know that some can be set so that they never pay off. Yet, he somehow feels that he will be the exception. Yes, others may lose, but he will win. Such customers give us a profit of billions of dollars a year in slot machines alone.

Compulsive gamblers are often very intelligent people, with strong drives for acceptance and success. Our strategy is to give them an early win that makes them believe that they are superior to others and can beat the odds. Their early "big win" so preoccupies them that they convince themselves that while others may lose, they will win. Gambling becomes a way to make themselves somebody. It is important that we hook them early, for the earlier in a person's life the gambling habit starts, the harder it will be to break later. The majority of compulsive gamblers began at about fourteen years of age.

Gamblers don't always become addicts immediately. It may take from five to twenty years to develop a real compulsive. Such a person eventually comes to the place that he is interested in nothing but our action. He has no other interests at all. He is unable to function without the excitement of gambling. He goes deeper and deeper into debt. He sleeps poorly and ignores his family, job, and friends. He often goes deeper and deeper into alcohol, and becomes tense and irritable. All he thinks about is the next bet—or taking his life.

Experts say that 99.9 per cent of all people who bet on the horses lose money steadily. But so well is our product marketed that our customers go to great lengths to have the privilege of giving us their earnings. The customer dreams of winning and thinks of all the things he will do with his winnings, while he cheerfully gives his money to our illusion field men who are only to glad to receive it.

It is true that we receive, on occasion, adverse publicity because of corruption in our athletic sales department. Occasionally some of our distributors have been brought into public disfavor. They made the unfortunate mistake of dealing with corrupt athletes who, rather than throwing their games, reported our distributors to athletic officials of the OPPOSITION's camp. It is to be hoped that in the future our men will refuse to do business with athletes who will not respect their confidence. I assure you, Mr. Chairman, that I am doing everything in my power to fix this problem.

We continue to direct the attention of the willing public to the amount of tax money we provide. We do not, of course, call attention to the cost to society that is being paid. The average compulsive gambler bets twice what he makes and costs society $40,000 a year. A 1975 Johns Hopkins report on compulsive gambling estimated that it costs our society over $28 billion annually. The personal cost is also impressive when you think that each compulsive gambler disrupts the life of ten to seventeen other people from among his friends, relative, creditors, and co-workers.

We have been so successful these past few years that the sociologist Edward Devereus has said, "A drastic increase in compulsive gambling has the makings of a major social and economic problem in the United States. It hasn't reached the magnitude of drugs or alcohol, but it could get to that point as wagering opportunities become more and more available." That, of course, is our hope for the future, Mr. Chairman.

In conclusion, I would like to say that we have succeeded in turning nearly every athletic event into profit and with a little bit of luck, if you will pardon the expression, the odds are that we shall continue to do so in the future.

MR. CHAIRMAN: Nothing would be a surer bet, my dear Ms. Ming. Your department is to be commended for its fine work. Now we want to hear from Mr. Nick O'Teen.

MR. NICK O'TEEN *(He is noticeably uneasy and nervous during his report. He is agitated and unsure of himself. He stammers occasionally when he becomes excited. His nervous gestures increase throughout his speech, though he frequently tries to control himself.):* Cigarettes continue to be our major seller, though tobacco in all its forms is a hot item, if you will excuse the pun. Through the years we have built a solid market for this once obscure weed. Our line started as a lowly spark and it has grown into a great conflagration *(nervous laugh)*. We continue to impress upon the public that our products are status symbols, that they are refreshing, and that they are pleasurable. We have lobbied for the right of our customers to use our products wherever and whenever they please.

Our success has been largely—I say, for the most part—due to the, eh,—fine product line developed by IVI's Development Department. It is not difficult to sell a—good product—I mean one in which you sincerely believe. *(He breaks here, unsure of himself. He stops often as if questioning the words that he is reading.)* That is the case with the Fashion line. They are sure-fire sellers. Man's crowd instinct gets him started.

Once a customer begins to take our products, we convince him that he can not get along without them.

I think you must appreciate the great difficulties under which our department works. First of all, we are faced with marketing a product, that when it is first used, brings sickness rather than pleasure. What other product must overcome such an initial contradiction to its advertising? It is to the credit of our sales force and the remarkable reasoning processes of man, that we are able to overcome this formidable barrier to sales.

I know that our department is not alone in these difficulties. I know that Mr. Cohol must have a similar problem in trying to present his respectability "pitch" to people who have seen his true customers drunk on skid row. I know that you, Ms. Ming, must deal with legal problems and adverse publicity because of the underworld figures that you rely on so heavily to promote your illusion. But sometimes I feel as if the whole scientific world is against *me*.

Excuse me for getting ahead of myself. I am happy to report that there are 53 million cigarette smokers in the United States. That means that between one in four and one in five Americans, including children, is hooked on our best selling tobacco product. That is the good news. The bad news is that the proportion of current smokers has declined from 1965 until now. Further, the per capita use of cigarettes has declined to the lowest level since 1957. Still, on the bright side, is the fact that the average smoker smokes about twenty cigarettes a day.

In 1982, our latest year for complete figures, Americans bought 711 billion cigarettes and 4.5 billion cigars. We continue our efforts to increase this volumne. We push tobacco products on television to the tune of $11 million a year and spend over $400 million annually on newspaper and magazine advertising to convince people that smoking is cool. We associate it with athletics, good times, and natural settings. We never, as your are well aware, show cancer wards or mortuaries in our ads, though the OPPOSITION has suggested that that would be a more accurate picture of our prod-

ucts. The figure that troubles me the most is that since 1964, 30 million people have quit smoking, almost all of them on their own, without elaborate programs. Quite frankly, I am disappointed with our Promotion Department. They must do more to perpetuate the idea that smoking is a habit that cannot be broken or our Pharmacology Department must make our products more addictive. Why, it is even being said by the OPPOSITION that the best way to quit smoking is to quit "cold turkey." Now if that should get out, we'll lose our hold on countless customers.

Now, where was I? Oh, yes, the future. We have hope, of course. A child who has at least one parent who smokes is about twice as likely to become a smoker than a child who does not have a parent who smokes. That is an encouraging figure, even though the schools are telling students it is no longer smart to smoke. It seems as if everyone is conspiring against us. . . .

Not even our best customers speak well of us. We always have been proud of our compulsive users, that wonderful, loyal band of chain smokers. Certainly we have established brand loyalty with them. But I still hear them telling people that they are sorry they started, that they want to quit, and that they know how harmful our "refreshing" habit is to their health and pocketbooks.

I don't mean to complain, but it is becoming a real war out there! It seems that we have enemies everywhere! The surgeon General is firmly on the side of the OPPOSITION. He had the temerity to say, as recently as 1982, "Cigarette smoking is clearly identified as the chief preventable cause of death in our society and the most important public health issue of our time." His 1979 report indicated that smoking is a major cause of cancer in the lung, mouth, and esophagus, and is a major contributing factor for the development of cancer of the bladder, pancreas, and kidney. They've even forced us to put warning labels on our packages and in our advertising—and they've barred us from public places—and . . . (*Shows signs of breaking down*).

(Taking control of himself.) Yes, as I was saying. It is becoming increasingly difficult to hide the illusionary nature of our business. We are being confronted with new evidence every day that links our products with lung cancer, heart disease, and with countless other diseases. We keep arguing that the evidence is not conclusive, but they keep piling up the scientific data against us. Take coronary heart disease, for example. They have done studies that have involved over 20 million person-years of observations and have concluded that smokers have a 70 per cent greater coronary heart disease death rate than non-smokers. Heavy smokers, those who smoke over two packs a day, have a mortality rate from coronary heart disease 200 percent greater than non-smokers. Why can't we come up with some sort of smoke screen to hide these facts from the public, I ask you? I can't pick up a newspaper or a magazine—even the ones we advertise in so heavily—that doesn't carry articles about how dangerous our products are to health. They call attention to the 129,000 premature deaths from heart disease that were attributed to smoking in 1982. Some even set the figure at 170,000 premature deaths each year from coronary heart disease attributed to smoking. They trumpet that over 94,000 lung cancer deaths each year are directly related to smoking. That means that every five and a half minutes a person dies of lung cancer related directly to smoking. They proclaim all this to the world. And what do we say? We say our products taste good. We say they satisfy. We say they are chic. It just won't cut it!

The Surgeon General says that cigarette smoking is the major single cause of cancer mortality in the United States, and what do we do? We show some girl in a bathing suit trying to keep her cigarette from getting wet while splashing in a swimming pool. Now really! That won't fool anyone. I mean really! When the OPPOSITION is publishing reports that cigarette smokers have a death rate two times greater than non-smokers and heavy smokers have a death rate three to four times greater than non-smokers? When smokers die of lung cancer ten times as often as nonsmokers? And heavy smokers die of lung cancer fifteen to twenty-five times more frequently than non-smokers? A girl in a bathing suit? A man on a horse? A fellow on a sailboat? Who are we kidding?

I thought for awhile that these problems would go away. Since nine out of ten lung cancer victims die within five years after diagnosis, I thought maybe we could bury these facts. But they just won't go away.

I'm even having trouble with the health industry. You'd think they'd be grateful to us. We provide them with $13 billion a year in smoking-related health care. But are they grateful? Not on your life. Doctors are the worst offenders. Whenever anyone gets sick the first thing they want our customers to do is give up our products. Don't they realize how much business we send their way? Why, from lung cancer alone, we provided physicians with $78 million in fees they would never have had had it not been from our cigarettes.

And the morticians are a silent lot as well. You'd think they would sponsor our advertising campaigns themselves, seeing as how much business we send them. But they are as quiet as the grave.

And think of all the new jobs we create for the economy. The OPPOSITION points out that at least $25 billion is lost in production and wages each year because of our tobacco products. Yet, each cancer death and heart attack opens up a job for an unemployed person. Does anybody praise us for that, I ask you?

The OPPOSITION tells everybody that to stop smoking is to increase their health and well-being. That may be true, but even its own reports say that it will take fifteen or twenty years of non-smoking for a person's risk of dying of lung cancer to return to that of a non-smoker. And it will take at least ten years for the risk of heart disease to return to that of non-smokers. No wonder so many people are saying "no" to the cigarette habit at the very start.

I contend that there is something basically wrong with our product or our marketing techniques. It is true that 4,000 different compounds have been identified in tobacco smoke.

The problem is that so many of them are harmful. And we're not doing nearly a good enough job of covering that up. Between 1965 and 1980 there were 3 billion premature deaths in America attributed to smoking. Now 340,000 deaths *each year* are linked with our tobacco industry and the public no longer believes we have their pleasure in mind when we market our products. If we are to maintain our present level of addiction in the U.S. population, we can expect that one out of every ten will die prematurely of heart disease attributable to smoking. We're killing off our best customers! How can we expect to increase our market that way. The total of premature deaths may exceed 24 million in the present population. That's a lot of customers to lose permanently. I don't know how you expect me to function in such circumstances.

Oh, we have been successful in introducing more women to our products since World War II. They've come a long way. They are approaching cancer and heart disease statistics that make them the equal of men. But here I'm having to cover up the fact that pregnant women who smoke have more miscarriages, premature births, and birth defects than women who don't. Surely you can't expect me to win against odds like that.

Recent studies have also indicated that nonsmokers who are forced to breathe the exhaust of our smokers are exposed to serious health hazards. I used to hold my head up high, confident that we had one of the best illusions going. But everywhere I look there seems to be smoldering discontent. Oh, we're still making plenty of money. However, our image is slipping drastically, despite all our ads that associate smoking with health and happiness: Sometimes, it is almost more than I can take!

(To the Chairman.) I'm sorry, sir. *(Back to the report.)* I don't mean to complain. I don't ask for your sympathy. I just want you to know how rough it is out there. I used to be able to say that the evidence just wasn't conclusive. I'd say that there had to be a lot of other factors in lung cancer and heart disease. Nobody believes me anymore. The evidence just keeps piling up.

Somehow, we've got to turn this thing around!

We are approaching a great crisis! I can't see through the smoke of the future, but I know that we are in trouble ...

MR. CHAIRMAN *(interrupting):* My dear Mr. Nick O'Teen, those are strong words indeed—very strong words. We have weathered such storms in the past. Your problem is that you are new to our management team. You do not recognize the holding power of a true illusion. You do not know your history. Man is perfectly capable of ignoring the facts you mention. We have abundant evidence that people just don't believe the awful things that are being said about your product line. They would rather believe our advertising with all its lovely mountains, cool streams, and beautiful, happy people than the facts and figures of scientific reports. They are too sophisticated for the scare tactics of the OPPOSITION with its emphasis on cancer wards and critical care units. You see, our customers have a wonderful ability to assume that they are exceptions, that they will not pay the cost in sickness for their "pleasure."

MR. NICK O'TEEN: Forgive me for getting so worked up, but what I said still stands. It is true that the consumers have been able to ignore these contradictions in the past. However, the OPPOSITION has been taking ruthless steps to blow holes in our smoke screen.

Though I am a new manager, I know that this is not the first time you have had problems with this product. I have noted a frequent change of managers in the tobacco division. Why, in 1954—

MR. CHAIRMAN *(interrupting):* Oh, yes, the year of the introduction of filter tips. Our tobacco man was very pleased with them, as I recall.

MR. NICK O'TEEN: Yes he was, at first. Volume jumped overnight. But then what happened? Consumers complained that the filters were so good that nothing came through but warm air. Everybody was mad at us. So the development boys loosened the filters and the consumers were happy again. Then the OPPOSITION conducted some tests and told the public our filter tip products were actually more harmful than the regular old lines had been. Don't talk to me about filters!

MR. CHAIRMAN (*studying him carefully*): You seem to take the OPPOSITION's tests very seriously....

MR. NICK O'TEEN: Not me, but the public does. I was going to talk about that later, but I guess this is as good a time as any to get it off my chest. I want help from the legal department. We've got to sue somebody for libel or something. People are always writing terrible things about this IVI product. They says it causes cancer, heart disease, and diminished eyesight, that it is a major cause of destructive fires, that it harms young people....

MR. CHAIRMAN: What's new about that? We've had that sort of publicity for decades, and we've always managed to survive. That's the beauty of a good illusion. Why even back in 1954 there was a report by Dr. E. Cuyler Hammond and Dr. Danile Horn of the Statistical Research Department of the American Cancer Society. They studied the habits of 187,766 men between the ages of fifty and seventy and found that smoking was related to an increase in the general death rate. Of 4,854 men who died during the course of that study, a total of 3,022 deaths occurred among regular cigarette smokers, the report said, only 1,980 deaths would have occurred. They said that even light smoking was associated with an increase in the death rate. Death rates were appreciably higher, they claimed, among light cigarette smokers than among non-smokers. They went so far as to assert that "Cigarette smoking is associated with an increase in the death rate for most of the more common sites of cancer in men." They went on to say that heavy smoking nearly doubles the death rate for diseases of coronary arteries and from cancer. They boldly asserted that there was a cause and effect rela-

tionship between smoking and the death rate. But did that sink us? Did that quench our fires? Not on your life! We've got to go on as if these things are never being said. A good smoke screen of advertising and counter claims will always get us through.

MR. NICK O'TEEN: But every year the weight of the evidence against us increases. Our products have provided lots of work for scientists. They say that 6,500-9,000 people die annually from smoking-related cancer of the mouth, 4,150 from smoking-related cancer of the esophagus, 6,000-8,000 from smoking-related cancer of the pancreas. Add to these all the deaths from lung cancer and heart disease and you can see what a tremendous contribution we are making to the arresting of the population explosion. Yet, sometimes I think nobody loves us. Something dramatic has to be done....

MR. CHAIRMAN: Now, Nick, don't get so excited.

MR. NICK O'TEEN: Don't get excited! Don't get excited! How do you expect me to act when our products are being raked over the coals? How can I continue if people find out the truth and give up our tobacco illusion? What kind of product are the Development people giving me anyway, when people can just go out and quit?

MR. CHAIRMAN: Our product people know their job, Nick.

MR. NICK O'TEEN: I need help! Why can't my products be as difficult to quit as Mary Wana's Pharmacology line? Then, no matter what the evidence, I'd still have a steady market.

MR. CHAIRMAN: We'll look into it.

MR. NICK O'TEEN (*belligerently*): You had better look into it, that's all I can say. I don't think you appreciate my problem. I don't think you appreciate it at all. How can I market a good illusion when people are always being reminded of reality?

MR. CHAIRMAN: Control yourself, O'Teen. Pull yourself together. I'm afraid the pace has been too much for you. You have made the unpardonable mistake of listening to the propaganda of the OPPOSITION. It has obviously unnerved you. I recommend that you spend a few weeks in the company rest home.

MR. NICK O'TEEN (becoming violent): I won't. There's nothing the matter with me that a little work and smoke won't cure. You're trying to get rid of me. That's it. Maybe you're working for the OPPOSITION. That's why the products haven't been good enough. That's why the Fashion Department hasn't met its goal. That's why the Legal department won't act. It's all your fault. (Chairman rings buzzer or bell. Two men come in and drag the now frantic MR. NICK O'TEEN from the room. They struggle with him.)

MR. CHAIRMAN (shaking head): This is indeed a sad moment for us all. Nick was one of our best men. It's too bad that he couldn't be content just to look at his sales figures. It's too bad to see a good man like that disintegrate. His mistake was listening to the propaganda of the OPPOSITION. Then he started to investigate his illusion—a practice we have warned all you IVI people about. Illusion-making is much too complicated for the unskilled. Your job is to sell, not to analyze. Nick began to examine his product and the attacks of the OPPOSITION drove him into shock. Let this be a lesson.

His third mistake was his loss of faith in human nature. He should have realized that all the studies in the world cannot drive a really first-class illusion from the market.

Now, for a bright spot. We have just enough time for a brief report from Ms. Mary Wana.

MS. MARY WANA: Our Pharmacology sales force has shown its usual substantial volume of trade. Our line includes Cocain, Benzedrine, Marijuana, Morphine, Codeine, and Heroin, among others. Marijuana continues to be our mainstay, though we have seen a dramatic rise in interest in cocaine. Nearly 43 million Americans have tried marijuana. Sixteen million are current users. A 1979 report indicates that about half a million high schoolers use it daily. Our annual sales are now somewhere in the area of $24 billion a year.

I am particularly glad to report that we are being successful in introducing the use of marijuana to the young. One out of seven 14-year-olds is a current user. One out of twenty-five 12-year-olds are getting hooked on the habit. I am pleased to report that over half the addicts are between twenty and thirty. I would also like to thank the Product Development department for giving us a much stronger marijuana than we were marketing in previous years. We have succeeded in thwarting a massive government attempt to put us out of business. We continue to spread the belief that marijuana is not addictive and to lobby for more liberalization of the laws dealing with marijuana use. We also do our best to discourage active prosecution. The product offers instant gratification and the illusion of well-being. We do not wish to publicize the fact that students who get hooked on marijuana often find their grades falling, and their interest in wholesome activities slipping. We have been particularly successful in our smoke screen of misinformation that has blinded young people to the medical evidence that marijuana is a dangerous drug that causes damage to the lungs, to the immunity system of the body and brain, and to the male and female reproductive systems. We have convinced them that marijuana usage does not lead to the use of more dangerous drugs, despite a recent study that indicated that one out of four daily pot users move on to heroin or other hard drugs, while only one in one hundred begin with the hard drugs. We are glad to report that marijuana is a perfect introduction to serious drug use. As the user builds up a tolerance to it, he requires more and more of it to get the "high" he seeks. Soon the user is not satisfied with marijuana and looks for something stronger to get the gratification he or she seeks. As one turns to drugs for pleasure and satisfaction, he ceases to develop normal channels for enjoyment. Drugs thus become a way of life. This is the goal of our marketing campaign.

Because of oppressive laws we are not permitted to advertise our products. But our products are so well designed that our customers become extremely loyal to them, even to the point of stealing to have money for their purchase. What a compliment to our research and development department!

I am particularly proud of the increase in our cocaine trade. One estimate is that one out of five Americans between 18-25 used it in 1979. Other estimates indicate that about 10 million Americans now use cocaine regularly and drug counselors estimate that from 5 per cent to 20 per cent, perhaps as high as 1 million are now hooked on it. That makes it nearly as popular a drug as heroin. Just during the last two years we have increased the number of Americans who have used cocaine from 15 to 20 million. Every day about 5,000 people sniff it for the first time. We market about 40 metric tons of cocaine a year.

Because of cocaine's expense, most of the users are in their 20's and 30's. A national survey indicated that one out of ten adults have sampled cocaine. We are pushing this drug deeper and deeper into the American life-style, though the federal government has mobilized 2,500 drug agents to cut into our trade. I am proud to report that cocaine is now nearly a $30 billion business, about three times as big as the recording and movie industries put together. I hate to brag, but some claim that cocaine is *the* most lucrative underworld business.

Cocaine has become a national epidemic, a compulsion for many who are willing to lose all to get it. Serious users have no conscience about breaking the law in obtaining it and passing it along to friends. One news magazine article calls cocaine the "perfect illusion," for "it makes people feel smarter, sexier and more competent, radiant, vigilant, masterful, *better:* it promotes a kind of fascism of the self." It makes people feel indestructible, powerful, and in control. That shows what a wonderful illusion it is. Though people are out of control, on the edge of ruin, and destroying themselves, they feel exactly the opposite. After the false sense of supremacy there comes a horrible crash which leads many to resort to other drugs of our product line, including heroin. Though cocaine was thought to be responsible for at least 300 deaths in 1981, we have been able to convince people that it will not harm them. We have suppressed evidence of the medical risk that is increasingly being documented about our products.

Our products continue to be very costly. In the case of cocaine, at least, that has contributed to its being a status symbol. The destructive nature of our products has been well documented by the research of the OPPOSITION, but I am happy to report that people love our illusions more than they love the truth. Our customers look for immediate gratification and we are glad to supply it, at a cost, of course. They are incapable of enduring the normal stresses and strains of life and are grateful to the instant highs our product supply them. We are convinced that they will not look ahead and see that we will enslave them. In short, we intend to expand and consolidate our operations.

In closing, I must give a word of thanks to the many criminals who have, through the years, assisted us so ably in our endeavors. It can truly be said that we would be nothing without them. Thank you.

MR. CHAIRMAN: We are sorry that you don't have more time to speak to us of your many adventurous activities, Ms. Wana. We are aware that yours is the most, shall we say, unconventional of our major illusions. We wish you continued success in your monumental enterprise. The loyalty to our products that you have developed is truly outstanding. We constantly hear of those who have given up their marriages, jobs, homes, fortunes, and careers to pursue your products. The risks are high in your line, but the profits to IVI are phenomenal.

In closing, I must mention my concern regarding Nick's crack-up. We are nevertheless encouraged with today's reports. Illusion Vendors Incorporated prospers and we feel that its future is bright. As long as men and women love illusion, we will be here to make a profit from them.

IDea BaNK
service Projects/social activities

Our *statements* show that your *interest* has been *compounding* in **THE "GOOD STUFF" IDEA BANK, FDIC** *(Fun, Dynamic, Imaginative, and Creative)*. We have continued to *stock pile* ideas from youth workers across the country. These *new entries* should bring you consistent *dividends* as your youth program *matures*.

Planning for service projects and social activities in these *changing* times can be very *taxing* on your creativity. This is our *principle* reason for making these *funds* (ideas) available to you. We encourage you to take advantage of these *assets* so you will have both service and *social security!*

If you have some unique ideas that have been *profitable* in your ministry to youth, we want to hear from you! We invite you to open your personal **IRA** *(Individual Resource Account)* so that others will be able to *capitalize* on your creativity. You can help increase our *book value* by sending your *deposit* (idea) to:

THE "GOOD STUFF" IDEA BANK, FDIC
c/o Standard Publishing Company
8121 Hamilton Avenue
Cincinnati, OH 45231

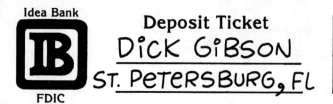

Idea Bank

IB

FDIC

Deposit Ticket
DICK GIBSON
ST. PETERSBURG, FL

Service Project	✕
Social Activity	
Net Deposit	"GOOD STUFF"

037

Secret Saints

The basic idea behind this service project is for the young people to be involved in doing things for other people in anonymous ways. They choose to do things for people that they do not know or may not be shown much love or appreciation.

Here are some ideas that have worked with our group: free car and window washes, baking cookies and taking them out to people, sending notes of love and encouragement using letters cut out from newspapers or magazines, gifts to new babies, lemonade run (taking drinks of lemonade to people working outside or caught in traffic jams), visiting nursing homes, doing something to show appreciation to our Bible School teachers or bus drivers.

This has been a project that has caught the attention and interest of many of our youth. It has helped us to think more about the needs of others and how to fill those needs in creative ways.

Idea Bank

IB

FDIC

Deposit Ticket
JEFF JACKSON
TULSA, OK

Service Project	✕
Social Activity	
Net Deposit	"GOOD STUFF"

038

Refugee Camp

This is an activity that our group did that helped heighten our awareness of the plight of most of the world's population.

We used our church camp facilities on a Friday night and Saturday. We let everyone relax the first evening in preparation for the next day. The next morning, we marched through the dorms at 6:00 a.m. gave instructions that everyone was to be outside, dressed and ready to go in 3 minutes. We transported everyone to a site on the camp grounds where we would spend the day. They were divided into groups of 8-10 and given cardboard boxes, ropes, and tarp to build a shelter. There was no breakfast or lunch, just a large drum of water in the center of the camp. We played some simulation games and had a 2 hour "boredom block." A truck arrived that evening to drop off some bags of rice. We cooked our supper (rice) in a central fire and talked about what the Bible says about the poor and the hungry and relating it to Matthew 25:40.

A program like this is available along with a film by writing "World Concern," Box 33000, Seatle, WA 98133. It helped change our group!

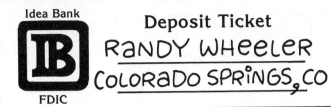

Service Project	✕	
Social Activity		
Net Deposit	"GOOD STUFF"	

Deposit Ticket

RANDY WHEELER
COLORADO SPRINGS, CO

039

P.E.T.S.

Our Jr.-Sr. High Service Project group is called P.E.T.S. (People Encouraging Through Service). This visitation group meets for 1½ hours each Wednesday. It takes practically no advance planning and is a great way to train kids in shepherding skills. We have a system of priorities for our visits.

1. *Hospital* -If anyone in the church or an acquaintance of a member is in the hospital, we make a large "Get Well" poster and take it to them. When we go to the hospital, we visit for just a few minutes, tape the poster on the wall, and pray with them.

2. *Birthdays and Anniversaries* -If no one is in the hospital, we check the church calendar for birthdays or anniversaries and we make appropriate posters. Then we stop at the respective homes, deliver the special poster, sing the song, and leave. (Continued.)

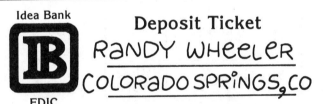

Service Project	✕	
Social Activity		
Net Deposit	"GOOD STUFF"	

Deposit Ticket

RANDY WHEELER
COLORADO SPRINGS, CO

040

P.E.T.S. (continued)

3. *Absentees*—If any of our teens have missed 4 weeks in a row, we make a large poster with faces all over it which says, "We Miss Your Face!" and surprise them at their home. Seventy-five percent of the time they'll be in church the next Sunday!

4. *Encouragement*—If no one fits the above categories on a given Wednesday night, we ask around to see if anyone is a little down or under stress. We make a poster that says, "We Love You!" When we deliver it, we visit for a few minutes and then leave.

P.E.T.S. has given our youth an opportunity to see how they can encourage others. It is fun for the youth, great "PR" for the youth group, and can be done with any size group of young people (we've made hospital calls with anywhere from 2 to 20 teens). Ours is a very low-key, relaxed group with little publicity, no arm twisting or recruitment. It is one of the most worthwhile things we do!

Idea Bank

IB

FDIC

Deposit Ticket

SCOTT HENNIG
GEORGETOWN, OH

Service Project	X
Social Activity	
Net Deposit	"GOOD STUFF"

041

Appreciation Night

We got our group involved in a special service project to show appreciation to some of the hardest workers in our church who are usually taken for granted—our Bible school teachers. Our young people were put in charge and they divided up the workload into several areas that would cover the preparations for the entire evening: invitations, table settings, menus, waiting on tables, food preparation, etc. The invitations were sent out two weeks prior to the event and reservations were required.

The fellowship hall was decorated beautifully and was lit by candles at each table and a few lamps. Soft Christian music was played in the background as the teachers and their spouses were seated at their romantic tables for two (card tables). The guests were then given fancy menus with such entrees as "veal cordon bleu," "fillet mignon," "broiled lobster tails," etc. But no matter what was ordered, everybody was served salad, spaghetti and meatballs, homemade garlic bread, and sherbet for dessert. The youth made it an elegant and delightful evening out and all of our teachers really felt appreciated!

Idea Bank

IB

FDIC

Deposit Ticket

DENNY STEVENSON
TIPTON, IN

Service Project	X
Social Activity	
Net Deposit	"GOOD STUFF"

042

Live Nativity Scene

Our young people participate in a live nativity scene at our church in celebration of Jesus birth. It is a project that requires the help of many people, but is very well received by the community.

Some of the men in our church have built a stable and manger to set the stage. People who own livestock have donated the use of an assortment of barnyard animals to be used to set the scene. Many of the women in our church have made costumes for all the characters of the nativity to wear that completes the look. When the parts are cast and the dates are chosen, the nativity begins.

We usually present the nativity in two different ways on two different nights. On one night, we just stand still in a posed position. The other night we walk through the scene with a reading of the Scripture every 20 minutes.

Our young people really enjoy doing this and the people of our community are reminded in a very special way of the coming of our Lord Jesus.

Idea Bank

IB

FDIC

Deposit Ticket

BiLL KOONTz
CiNCiNNaTi, OH

Service Project	X
Social Activity	
Net Deposit	"GOOD STUFF"

043

Commandos for Christ

For this service project, we have our young people meet at the church. They are instructed to wear all black clothing and to bring several paper bags. When everyone has arrived, we read Matthew 25:31-40. The concept of this project is to help those who are in need in tangible ways.

First, we load up in vans and go out to upper-middle class neighborhoods and ask for donations of food items to be given to the needy. We may spend anywhere from 30 minutes to an hour gathering these items. Then, we divide the gathered foods into the paper bags making sure there is a variety of items in each bag. Finally, we deliver the bags to the homes of needy families. We leave the bags on the doorsteps and run! There is a note attached to each bag that reads, "From the Commandos for Christ, God Bless You!"

Our young people really enjoy this project because of the immediate sense of accomplishment they receive!

Idea Bank

IB

FDIC

Deposit Ticket

JOHN Haak
ARLiNGTON, TX

Service Project	X
Social Activity	
Net Deposit	"GOOD STUFF"

044

Mission: IMPORTANT

Because families are more mobile now than in years past, it is not unusual for our young people to have many new students coming to their schools each year. Many times it is difficult for these newcomers to feel accepted by their new peers. To help meet this need, we initiated "Mission: IMPORTANT!"

The assignment for our young people (if they decided to accept it) was to seek out these new students in their schools. They were challenged to make them feel welcome in their new community and to help "show them the ropes" around school. The main concept was to be a friend to these newcomers in whatever way they could, and help them feel apart of things.

Naturally, "Mission: IMPORTANT" has led to many lasting friendships and has helped give our young people an opportunity to share their faith in positive and constructive ways.

Idea Bank

FDIC

Deposit Ticket
BRENT BROMSTRUP
BARRINGTON, R. I

Service Project	X
Social Activity	
Net Deposit	"GOOD STUFF"

045

Christmas Celebration

Our group participated in a different kind of Christmas celebration that really met some needs in our city. We combined efforts with the Salvation Army to host a Christmas Celebration for some young people who lived in the inner-city.

We spent some time in gathering up some gifts in many different ways. Some baked dozens of cookies while others went to different businesses asking for donations of items that could be given to the needy. We also coordinated a program for this special event.

When all was ready, we met for about a 2½ hour program in which we lead everyone in some games, singing, skits, and teaching. Then we shared in a time of gift giving while we ate the cookies some of our young people made. It was a Christmas celebration that our group will remember for a long time to come!

Idea Bank

FDIC

Deposit Ticket
RICK TRAUTMAN
WHEATON, IL

Service Project	X
Social Activity	
Net Deposit	"GOOD STUFF"

046

Spring Work Trip

In the springtime, we take our junior high group out on a work trip of some sort to allow them an opportunity to participate in some meaningful service to others. One trip that was particularly special was when we went to work at a camp for handicapped kids in preparation for the season to come.

We participated in various types of work at the camp. There was plenty of physical labor such as cutting up some trees into firewood and clearing some rocks out of the fields. We also painted some picnic tables and generally helped out in any way we could.

This was a very good trip for our group in many ways. By working around the cage swings, the wide doors, the free space in the rooms, they were able to gain a greater awareness of the handicapped. At the conclusion of the trip, we talked about the importance of being doers of the Word and not hearers only.

Idea Bank

B

FDIC

Deposit Ticket

HANK SANFORD

CHAMPAIGN, IL

Service Project	
Social Activity	X
Net Deposit	"GOOD STUFF"

047

The Clue Game

We set up a "live" clue game very similar to the board game. The object of the game is to find out who was the murderer, what was the weapon, and where. The teens find this out by splitting into groups small enough to fit in a car. The cars are driven by sponsors to the houses of various witnesses. The witnesses are people from your church who have volunteered their help for the evening. Each witness only knows one piece of information except for two who know nothing at all. When a car arrives at the house of a witness, the teens may ask no more than two "yes" or "no" questions. They must record their answers and go ask questions at another house before they can return to the same house to ask more questions. When a team thinks they have solved the mystery, they go to an appointed house to see if they have the correct answers. You will want to provide a "clue" checklist on which the teams may record their information. You may want to consult the board game for further details or ideas.

Idea Bank

B

FDIC

Deposit Ticket

TOM RUTHERFORD

NASHVILLE, TN

Service Project	
Social Activity	X
Net Deposit	"GOOD STUFF"

048

All Saints Night

There are a lot of Christians who have a hard time dealing with the celebration of Halloween. Many in our church go through this dilema every year. We have offered our young people some more acceptable alternatives for the typical festivities of the evening.

Our approach has been to host an *All Saints Night,* a party on Ocotber 31 that celebrates our heritage in Jesus as opposed to celebrating with demons and witches. We've done this for the last 6 years in a variety of ways. It's always a costume party, sometimes dressing as Bible characters and other times letting them dress in whatever way they want providing it is not of the evil and scary variety. Activities have included trick-or-treating for UNICEF, the bobbing for apples and eating powdered donuts on a string type games, etc. One year we even tried a two part social by hosting a party for some little kids for the first part of the evening and then having our own. We have had a lot of good response for this activity from the youth and their parents alike!

Idea Bank

IB

FDIC

Deposit Ticket

MaRK SHaNeR
Lake WHaLeS, FL

Service Project	
Social Activity	X
Net Deposit	"GOOD STUFF"

049

Son Rise Celebration

After the high school prom, many couples in our area go out for breakfast or go to a parent's home where a breakfast is served. We use this as a creative time to provide a healthy atmosphere following the prom.

We have all our high school youth workers come to the church dressed in formals and tuxedos while the prom is still in full swing. We prepare a massive breakfast at the church to be served shortly after the prom is officially over. When the young people arrive, we begin serving the food! Following the breakfast we have a light program prepared featuring some contemporary Christian music videos, songs, and devotions.

This is now an annual event that we look forward to each year. Maybe your group members would enjoy it, too!

Idea Bank

IB

FDIC

Deposit Ticket

RiDGe BURNS
WHeaTON, IL

Service Project	
Social Activity	X
Net Deposit	"GOOD STUFF"

050

Super Stars

This is a all day event that we do in our community. It is an excellent evangelistic tool to bring young people out for some wholesome activities—young people that may be reluctant to come to church when first invited.

We model our program after the TV show "Almost Anything Goes." The main idea is to get the young people involved in some low skill games. We do this by meeting in a large field. When everyone arrives, we divide them into teams of 5 or 6 players and 1 coach. All day we have some competition in some crazy low skill games. Everyone competes with his or her team and the team points are tallied throughout the day. Some of our games have included the following: how many nails can a team drive into a board in 3 minutes, how many times can a team volley a volleyball in a circle, walking on a balance beam, a frisbee toss, and many relay races like trying to fill a bucket at the far end of a field with water by carrying a small cup at a time from the other end of the field. These activities provide lots of fun in a non-threatening environment, especially for new young people you are trying to reach.

Idea Bank

FDIC

Deposit Ticket
KEVIN KLEIN
JOPLIN, MO

Service Project	
Social Activity	X
Net Deposit	"GOOD STUFF"

051

Parent/Teen Progressive Dinner

This was an activity we did with our junior high young people and one of their parents. When everyone arrived at the church, each teen and parent were handcuffed together (toy handcuffs) and given a sheriff's badge for the evening. They were instructed that each person would take turns being "boss" (wearing the badge) for 15 minutes, and then the other person would be the "boss." Every decision that the "boss" made had to be in the best interest of the "servant." Then, we proceeded on the bus to begin our progressive dinner including stops for appetizers, sandwiches, chips and vegetables, and dessert. All the food was arranged in a self-service manner, so that each handcuffed pair had to work together to fix and eat their food. Following the dessert, we played some games still handcuffed. Finally, we shared in a devotional time discussing the subject of authority. The implications were clear for both parents and teens regarding the responsibilities of leadership and submission. It has been one of the most significant things we have done all year!

Idea Bank

FDIC

Deposit Ticket
PAUL BORTHWICK
LEXINGTON, MA

Service Project	
Social Activity	X
Net Deposit	"GOOD STUFF"

052

Fantasty Island Night

This was a fun social event that was a take off of the TV show, *"Fantasy Island."* In this social, we were not only able to have a good time together, but we also learned about some things that were important to each member of the group.

In preparation for this activity, everyone was told that they must come dressed in an outfit and/or with props that would express to the rest of the group a dream or fantasy they had for their future. When the young people arrived, they were welcomed by Mr. Rork and Tatoo (some of our sponsors) dressed up in white suits. We had some games, relays, and refreshments of the island variety. Then towards the end of the evening, we had a time where each person shared with the group about their dream or fantasy for which they came dressed that evening.

Idea Bank

IB

FDIC

Deposit Ticket

Tom Rutherford

Nashville, TN

Service Project	
Social Activity	✕
Net Deposit	"Good Stuff"

053

F.B.I.

F.B.I. stands for "Finding Bodies Immediately." It's a game where the youth have to find their disguised youth leaders in a crowded place. We break the group into teams of 4 or 5 and give them pictures of the leaders as they appear in real life. In the meantime, the leaders have done anything they can to disguise themselves using clothing, wigs, false beards, make-up, etc., and have gone ahead of the group to the designated place (we like to use a shopping mall). Each leader has cards with varying amounts of points on them. The first team to find each leader gets a card worth 1,000 points; the second is worth 500; the third is worth 300; etc. As the teams roam through the mall and think they recognize one of the leaders, they must ask the person, "Are you on the F.B.I.'s wanted list?" If the person is one of your leaders, he/she gives the group the card indicated the number of points they have earned. If the person is not one of the youth leaders, it creates an hilarious situation where the team members have to explain what they are doing. Have a designated place to meet the leaders after the playing time is over.

Idea Bank

IB

FDIC

Deposit Ticket

Jay St. Clair

Joplin, MO

Service Project	
Social Activity	✕
Net Deposit	"Good Stuff"

054

Saturday Night at the Movies

At the beginning of the evening we played a mixer game that introduced the theme of the evening. Then we settled down to watch a video prepared by the members of our group to introduce the feature film. The video was called *What Went Wong at Wamat?* (Walmart). It was a spoof of the TV show "Kung Foo" that was popular a few years ago. The main character, Grasscatcher, was warned by his Master to stay away from the red-light specials at *Wamat* so he wouldn't be trampled in the stampede. Reluctant to follow his instructions, Grasscatcher went to *Wamat* and was trampled. The 35 minute video was sprinkled with spoofs of popular commercials with spiritual applications (i.e., Where's the Beef?—spiritual food). Our young people did all the production and it was great. This was followed by our feature film called *Never Ashamed* which related the struggles of a young man trying to grow in his new found faith. During the film, we served popcorn and softdrinks. After the film, we had a live visit from Grasscatcher and his Master who divided us into discussion groups to discuss the application of the film.

Other Resources for Youth Leaders

Ministering to Youth, *edited by David Roadcup.* #88582

A total approach to youth ministry combining theoretical and practical information. It begins with a discussion of the development of the "youth culture" in this century; then a look at the youth minister himself, his personal life, and his relationship with God.

Methods for Youth Ministry, *edited by David Roadcup.* #88589

This book is a useful tool for anyone who ministers to the needs of young people. Building on the same philosophy as *Ministry to Youth,* the writers of this book offer solid, practical suggestions for conducting a variety of events and reaching important goals.

"GOOD STUFF"—Resources for Youth Leaders. #3403, #3407

"GOOD STUFF" is a series of resource books for leaders of Junior and Senior High teens. Each book contains four topical studies loaded with resource materials, learning activities, worksheets, and transparencies. The studies are flexible enough to be used in weekly youth meetings, retreats, etc. Watch for future volumes.

You Can Teach Teens Successfully! *by Roy Reiswig.* #3207

This book will equip you for success in the classroom. The author shares information in the following areas: the role of the teacher, the role of the Bible in teaching, teenagers—Who? What? Why?, lesson planning, classroom management, and methods of teaching.

Dating & Waiting: A Christian View of Love, Sex, and Dating, *by Les Christie.* #39972

"How to" advice for youth: how to get a date, where to go, what to do, how to set standards, how to deal with the "heavy issues" of dating. It is designed not to preach, but to help teens come to an understanding about Christian dating.

Christian Ways to Date, Go Steady, and Break Up, *by John Butler.* #39949

Covers nearly every facet dating, from casual acquaintance, to going steady, to the difficulty of ending a relationship. Positive, sympathetic—concerned with what to do and how to do it.

Available at your Christian bookstore or

STANDARD® PUBLISHING